BIPOLAR IS NOT AN STD

Beyond Bipolar Anxiety, Depression, Personality Problems, and Relationship Offenses

DR. LAUREN GOODALL

Bipolar Is Not an STD

Beyond Bipolar, anxiety, depression, personality problems, and relationship offenses

Dr. Lauren Goodall

ISBN (Print Edition): 978-1-08940-150-6

About You:

You probably haven't had the easiest life, and you may be wondering if life is really worth putting effort into. Maybe you have been repeatedly let down by another person. Maybe you just want to have a relationship; but all you find is a relationship with relationships…as in plural. Not what you had in mind. Maybe you battle against depression. Maybe it is anxiety that you're trying to fight. Maybe you get angry. Maybe you battle drugs. Maybe your biggest battle is within yourself.

People don't often bet on others, but I believe in the strength of the human spirit to overcome an unbeatable path. You move forward even with big doubt. Your journey matters, and it's not about beginnings it's about how you navigate through tough spaces, but most importantly, it's how you land it. I know how to land stuff in the dark, with broken flight gear; so I know that it can be done.

My starting point in Psychology was an Ending:

When you get to the hospital, the Emergency staff is awkward, because they know that your person is dead. They just transport the body and inform the family when they arrive. I bolted into THAT room to try attending to someone who couldn't be attended to—to try to talk to someone who couldn't be talked to. Me and my nightmare of loss, which haunted me for most of my life, was being alone in that room with a dead, going cold body that I couldn't fix. The main person I counted on, was a big person, with an unfortunately big addiction. I hung over a dead body; trying to make some kind of desperate plea deal that could not be made. I don't know who had more demons at the time, him or me. However, it's hard to avoid inner demons. Demons aren't hard to acquire—demons of comparison, demons of less than, and demons of being completely alone. When you have something to prove to yourself, you work all the time. So that's what I did. In order to be any good at working in the field of Psychology, I had to have some basis of understanding hell. That wasn't hard to come by.

I am grateful for all the clients whom I've met and hopefully honored in our sessions. I'm grateful to the front line of people, who have worked and coordinated with me professionally and personally. We shared ideas and intellectual space. From Psychologists, to doctors and lawyers—we were out to help our people, and I think we did. Across space and time, the people on that path mattered.

> "Life is about finding how far you can go, how fast you can run, and you never know until you try.
> Until you run."
>
> - Secretariat "Making of a Champion," Randall Wallace.

The problem isn't starting out, it is fighting for time. You set a course and get re-routed. Perhaps your GPS broke a long time ago. You are now flying without instrument. Sometimes you have nothing. No external gauges to help. No person or outside influence. You know that you have to do the run. The run is the only thing left to do. This book is for anyone who had to run a race that they didn't think they had in them. Whether it was your second broken marriage, your kid in the jail cell, your cancer, your fleet of mobile rage—let's face it, this wasn't supposed to be your race. But now it IS. Yet for every reason that you have to not run, there's one that supersedes it. If you run this race, you get to beat the inner voice that's been crapping all over your living space. For that reason alone, the race is worthy. For that reason alone, you will get dirty. Don't get sidetracked by the dirt, it's just a distraction. Keep your eyes fixed up and forward. You were invited to the track because you are a warrior. You got the heavy assignment because you can run it.

My Background:

I have worked in the mental health field for 24 years as a Psychologist. I believe in effective therapy. Effective therapy is not seeing a person for several years. A better phrase for that is an "ongoing" or "incomplete" dialogue. With my work, I wanted to get people better faster. Life is hard enough. So, I also consulted with others—Psychiatrists and Physician colleagues. I had my own private practice office where I worked with probably every form of mental illness, including depression, anxiety, panic, or Bipolar disorder. The most rewarding part was in being able to get better than average results. In my early years, I worked in a private psychiatric hospital working with most types of severity of mental illness from children to adults, from psychosis to neurosis. I excelled in differential diagnosis, which means understanding the fine distinctions that separate disorders. I didn't like test results that gave people a list of diagnosis; I didn't find that accurate. I knew what tests could do, and what they could not. So, I was good at the defense aspect, of not buying into everything a computerized assessment showed. Later, I did clinical review of cases to make sure the cases were targeted clinically, or in standard words, for therapy effectiveness, Utilization review, and larger group supervision. I also published and testified. I've worked the last eight years, in private settings with women nationally and internationally from every walk of life.

Cracking the Code: Mental vs. Medical

I also believe that the reason some people don't get better and stay better, is that there are underlying MEDICAL factors that trigger and cause mood symptoms such as severe depression, anxiety, or Bipolar. For many, psychological symptoms are rooted in a situation or the environment they were raised in. That's fine, and that will always be a factor. However, for others, the psychological agitation or upset was started by the brain's cell messengers that over-reacted or under-reacted leaving a person feeling miserable or ready to jump out of their skin. Because of this MEDICAL chemical reaction or sub-par response, the person will have a much more difficult time "snapping out of it." This book is for people who want to know what causes this and how to shut this system problem down faster.

When you know what is happening in the body as a whole, it makes your therapy work much faster. I'm not a fan of doing therapy for years. If you are, it's likely that some of the root causes of your issues haven't been treated effectively. And remember, more of the same dialogue isn't going to be the answer.

You may need to reach, research, and study a bit to get your answers. But there is nothing more rewarding when your brain and body can exist in harmony. I believe you can get better and faster and have a better quality of life. But you need a better understanding of what is happening to understand your symptoms and reboot your life.

To Treat It Or Hide It:

This book is for the people who have the courage to recognize that something isn't quite right and want to get better. In the generations before us, people were afraid to address their mental health for fear of being called crazy, which produced endless bad outcomes. The person not only does damage to themselves, but also their families. The purpose of this book is to educate others to understand the biology of the brain of how and why some people experience more psychological symptoms than others. Depression, anxiety, and Bipolar disorders don't happen because people are "weak." There are plenty of high powered, successful people experiencing all of this. So, let's get this part straight.

Persons with mood disorders are strong because they are distance runners. When you have a medical factor imposing, the medical aspect undoubtedly will make it harder. Weak is not part of the equation. At their core, medical factors and chronic stress trigger psychological symptoms. Medical factors need to be managed. The first step in the management is recognizing the factors. I respect the people are struggling with mental illnesses. It's a lot harder for them, and they didn't ask for it anymore than a patient who has high cholesterol. They too wake up and play ball with it and join millions who experience these same types of symptoms. That takes guts.

Medical factors affect the body in the same manner as when a body gradually develops disease, breaks down with exhaustion, or when it has the flu. The brain has wiring that will influence chemical information processing. To be clear, I believe a lot of Psychological symptom distress begins with chemical and communication fluctuations in the brain, that secondarily produces a great deal of psychological distress. People don't choose the symptoms. The biology of symptoms can lead us to the root.

Some stress is situational. Other stress adds to an already upset or overly reactive system. I don't believe that changing your thinking to feel better is a very simple process. It might work for some, but for others, a more technical understanding of how the body works and how it fails is required.

Don't Bake the Cake Backwards:

I believe the brain reads, transcribes, and responds to gene codes as well as environmental stressors that trigger physiological responses and physical changes in a person's internal sense of well being. If you are unsure of that, just meet a person with Post-Traumatic Stress Disorder. Their internal biochemistry has been dismantled so deeply that what others see is a very disturbed sleep full of live nightmares, waking to severe agitation, which becomes evidenced through their hyper-reactive or over-reaction to situations. So biology can attack a person, like a rabid dog, and start facilitating bad or over-reactive responses to otherwise benign threats. To help these people get better, you have to find multiple different ways to re-level the chemistry to stop the hyper-firing, and then you can work on neutralizing thought associations that maintain or trigger the firing. If you do it backwards—by talking to someone whose agitation is in the stratosphere, then they cannot focus on you or respond to you because of chemical and mental aspects co-firing. Therefore, focus should be on body chemistry first, and then neutralize the thought process. You can't bake the cake backwards. It will not work.

As it stands, I'm not a true fan of the term mental illness. As long as the brain has bias on the body, the term mental health is a misnomer. It's like saying that pushing the accelerator has nothing to do with driving speed. The term mental health is used to be specific about where the symptoms are evidencing at the time i.e. thought process, emotions, or behavior. If these symptoms are not effectively treated, then your body manifests physical illness like Fibromyalgia, Lupus, autoimmune disorders, etc. For this book's purposes, the brain is viewed as the smooth or broken interaction of its electrical, hormonal, and chemical neurotransmitters' ability to stay within a certain functional range. The brain uses multiple equations of hormones, enzymes, endocrine system, sympathetic/parasympathetic systems, and intricate subsystems to function effectively. The "mental" part is a very integral effect of these various equations. Psychological distress is an output of the equation. Treating mental health issues without understanding this system produces results that don't stick.

Calling it Mental Health:

Once mental health was labeled, many people wanted no part of the label. We have generations of relatives before us who avoided that kind of help. Labels have some organizational purpose, but they end up creating bigger problems than there were at the beginning. In my opinion, good therapy involves examining both the underlying biological and psychological aspects. I believe that you have to have a strong knowledge of biological information systems as well as psychological factors and influences. Good therapy isn't just a form of advice. Your neighbor or your church can do that for you. Good therapy rests on physiological knowledge and psychological influences and symptoms. So, "changing your thinking," which is heavily marketed, albeit a nice concept, is TOO simplified. It can rarely stick in an effective manner if you have any susceptibility (even situationally) to biochemical or genetic factors that cause biochemical valleys, mini-spikes, or large spikes in brain chemicals (neurotransmitters) that are supposed to stay fixed to feel better.

Outcomes tell the story, so let's talk for a minute about bad outcomes.

An example of a bad outcome is Aunt Edna. She was in therapy for years and was put on all sorts of medication—likely misdiagnosed—and she does not leave the house. Bad outcome.

Another bad outcome is found in young children (not toddlers) who throw terrible tantrums, hit themselves, and scream and get very angry or aggressive. If there isn't poor parenting or bad environment, the child's behavior isn't simply "bad." Their distress can be seen on their face, their screams, or cries. It is incorrect to write it off as just bad behavior.

Another bad outcome is assuming that young children are not capable of wanting to kill themselves. "Children and Suicide: Are there Red Flags to Look For?" *PSYCOM.net*, Hurley, Katie, LCSW, Updated 10/23/18, "suicide is the second leading cause of death in people ages 10-24." Pediatrics research publication also discusses the research findings, among them poor "relationship issues with family and friends," What this means is that children who lack good emotional support or attention, are going to be at risk for not wanting to live anymore. Children with suicidal behavior were more likely to experience "Attention deficit disorder, with or without hyperactivity." ("Children and Suicide: Are there Red Flags to Look For?" *PSYCOM.net*, Hurley, Katie, LCSW, 10/2318). What this means to me as a clinician, is that parts of ADHD, may put a child at risk; such as an impulsive trait. Children versus adolescence shows that "Adolescence were more likely to experience depression or dysthymia" (See above citation), as part of suicidal risk patterns. Multiple risk patterns forge the potential for suicidal types of behavior. Bad Outcome.

Substance abuse or prescription abuse. Bad outcome.

Onslaught of legal problems. Bad outcome

Multiple relationship failures—people who change partners but cannot or do not stay in a relationship for longer periods of time. Bad outcome.

These are just some signs in our society that indicate that something more is going on in the picture. It requires a closer look.

In order to do effective therapy with someone, you need to understand the chemical factors involved in the brain. If you don't understand that, then you end up with people who are in therapy for years with little improvement to show for it. As a Clinical Psychologist, it mattered to me that my people got better in a timely format. If I wasn't getting it right, then I wanted to find out what I was missing. That quest linked me with professionals who were able to recognize symptoms as viable symptoms BEFORE there was research data to support it. They were outliers in the field who thought out of the box. Basically, they learned from their clients because the textbooks didn't find the solution. I am forever grateful for the opportunity to work with those professionals. I am also very grateful to my clients, who gave me the understanding and motivation to seek better outcomes. If you are not asking questions, then it is likely that you are stagnating. Since I was able to do work with professionals who saw symptoms before they were ever published, I was able to do better than mediocre work with my clients.

Agendas behind Labeling:

The term "mental" did more damage than good. It caused people to go underground for fear of a label or being "locked up." Most generations have gone untreated for fear of being labeled "mental." There were years when a person could get institutionalized or called "crazy" and the person was placed in asylums. What was worse was that sometimes there were other motives in play. For instance, a husband wanted a divorce, so he states his wife is crazy. These days that agenda would never work. There are far more checks and balances in place. Just because someone wants to call you crazy, doesn't mean you are. The term crazy is just a form of slander, when you don't know what really is going on. However, the stereotypes breed and create loads of bad information. The poor methodology used in the past led people to avoid treatment all together. Instead, they just usually drank excessively, used amphetamines, or smoked pot to ease their suffering. But, really no one was ever diagnosed with depression, anxiety, or Bipolar. They just compensated by using whatever substance that could temporarily Band-Aid the condition. So now, when a client is asked about whether or not there are any family members diagnosed with psychiatric conditions, often, the answer is no. No is not because it isn't true. It isn't, because it's similar to asking about STD's. The world is full of them, but nobody knows if they have them or have had them in the past. So, using verbal family history to understand mental health is marginal for two reasons. The first is that most people do not know of emotional issues or behaviors that relatives engaged in due to denial, embarrassment, ignorance, or just wanting to present a positive look to the therapist. Agendas can mess up a diagnosis and treatment as much as anything. Perfectionists and social climbers, as in parents or clients, usually need a boat load of trust and non-judgment before they can even TRY to examine these issues. With these factors in mind, family history can be factored in, but NOT assumed as fact. The therapist often is left with very little real information to work with.

Secondly, what I find is that our templates aren't exact.

(If you are one of those "all or nothing category" finders, then you have come to the wrong place. You will not be happy with the conceptualization and frame that I provide. It will raise more questions than answers for you. If you need black and white clarity, then you will not find it here. For those of you looking for that, this is a good exit point).

Being good with checklist diagnosis doesn't make you right or good:

To be really good, as a therapist, we have to be willing to make mental distinctions and modifications based on existing information. If the clinician is interested in making the perfect diagnosis according to theory;they may miss the entire nuance of the disorder. By nuance, I am referring to the pitch, tone, rate, and style of information the client provides. A picture is worth a thousand words. You not only can describe features of a disorder, but you start putting together the subtleties of the disorder. You can walk it. On the other hand, researchers tend to obtain more information that pulls out the standard features.

Subtleties are not where researchers or accountants play ball. They only want the hard facts; the hard lines; the black and white. The ball field that clinicians play in is much more vast than those lines. Therefore, a clinician's skill is in finding that part of the criterion that isn't always accurate or modifies. There is a huge difference between theory and application.

Unfortunately, most people believe that all tests are accurate. People don't know that there is always a certain degree of error that a provider has to factor in. Because something is scientific—meaning made use of scientific method, does not make it accurate. Most people don't truly understand that tests, even good tests, can provide false positives and false negatives. What that means is that something may look like something, but it isn't that or the test could state that you don't have something, when you do. Much of that in clinician's work is only as good as the clinician's ability to recognize the front appearance of the disorder, as well as it's mini subparts. This is much more than a checklist on a page. It's like coding for computers. The IT person can recognize that the program looks structurally sound, however, there may be a virus that interferes with its application. The virus most commonly seen for medical professionals is "I've never seen it present like this," or "It's not diagnostically listed like this!" It is even more challenging when the researchers dictate the testing through one style of research. Keep in mind, there are false positives and false negatives in scientific research and testing. The occurrence of such an error can impact the overall effectiveness of medications chosen and therapy modules used for a client. When research information matches clinical presentation, you have a beautiful mosaic.

However, when they do not—as in when the clinician sees a different picture than the template that the researcher or statistician is using—there will be the problem. At those times, there is no mosaic, and we have to dig deeper for different types of information. However, clinicians have ways of meting out the information through a variety of methods that don't rely on the accuracy of one test. High praise to any professional who knows the limitations of computerized assessment. Because most people (professionals) unfortunately think of it as gospel. It is not. People have been shredded by computerized assessment at the hands of new and old professionals who really don't understand the limitations the gathered research, subjects, age demographics, and presentation. You have to know what goes into the test. For instance, what are the factors, loading markers, or scales, that point out what you are specifically trying to measure? Once you know these factors, it is easier to interpret where the errors may lie. Statistics are numbers, and numbers need interpretation. Therefore, statistics and research have scientific and clinical limitations and are also prone to error. Unfortunately many are led astray by this lack of knowledge.

An example, the puppy I got from a rescue became violently ill within 48 hours. Some people might say that it was due to transitional issues. My puppy exhibited vomiting and diarrhea, and the vet office wanted to rule out Parvo (a deadly dog disease). Both the first and second tests came out negative for Parvo. They tried a different intervention, and he did not respond or improve. Finally, the nurse said that just because it didn't test out, does not mean he doesn't have the disease. Thankfully, the vet nurse knew that the symptoms outweighed what the tests were sensitive to. When the vet followed the symptom profile, instead of the test, my puppy was treated for Parvo and got better. This is an example of a false negative. Where the test says you don't have it, but the test is not able to accurately pick it up, and you are actually positive. If she would have insisted that she would only follow the test; it is likely that my puppy would have died.

Another example of scientific error, comes from the movie, *The Dallas Buyers Club*, this is a movie, based on a true story, about the AIDS epidemic in the 80's. Doctors were treating the virus with what the pharmaceutical companies were directing. The people taking the medication (which was too strong) ended up dying shortly within the trial. It took an electrician who got the disease to start researching outside the given treatment. He fought his doctor's approach and went to different countries to see what other vitamins/medications were in use for his symptom profile. When he did so, every professional organization came against him—the FDA, the pharmaceutical companies, etc. However, he introduced longevity into the life of millions by finding vitamin supplements and treatments that could keep HIV from developing into AIDS.

The message here is NOT to ignore doctors or authority. The message is that sometimes the authority is wrong and you have to do your own research and pose the questions.

So You Think Computerized Data Is Always Right:

Now, think about computerized dating matches. Sometimes people look great on paper, and the computer identified you as a perfect fit, but when you meet the person, you have no interest. How do you explain that? The computer says you are great. What could it possibly have missed? Chemistry? You can't black and white a descriptor that will guarantee attraction. Chemistry is nuanced. So, it would be fair to say that there are people who have been date matched, that never hit it off. They were supposed to, by all other indicators, but somehow did not become a match. That would be an example of a false positive assessment. Computerized research is not bullet proof.

What is Bipolar?

Bipolar is a subject that most people have a loose grasp of. Many (including doctors) are still using an old template that doesn't work. Most people don't have periods of highs, followed by periods of lows. Those symptoms indicate traditional Bipolar—we now call it Bipolar I. Bipolar I is fairly easy to spot and recognize as the public has become more aware. People will tell you horror stories that the person is irresponsible, lazy, doesn't get to work on time, drinks too much, gets argumentative, doesn't sleep, or sleeps all the time. What ends up happening is that we put character labels on an illness that is hugely a medical condition.

If you ask someone on the street what they think a person with Bipolar acts like, then you tend to get answers that are stereotypes. Stereotyped messages are rarely accurate and have never healed anyone. Remember what happened to children before ADHD was considered a legitimate diagnosis? ? Well, because of their inability to sit in a chair all day for school, inability to follow through with schoolwork, they were considered to be stupid and have discipline problems. Often they were given physical punishment to "straighten them out" from paddles at school to paddles at home. They were often predicted to never make it in life. As we now know, nothing can be further than the truth. These folks may have attention problems, but they can be brilliant and very successful. They just need to accommodate for their area of limitation. It's hard to believe that we were ever stuck in the dark ages with this diagnosis, but we were.

Another dark age limitation we had was diagnosing a spectrum for Autistic Disorders. Decades ago, it was one size fits all. Your child may be gifted as an idiot savant, who can be a genius with numbers, but lags behind on more basic developmental milestones, such as speech or potty training. This fell under the category of Autism. However, the Autism category was too broad, and brought in an entirely different presentation we now call Asperger's disorder. A person with Asperger's disorder, largely functions through the use of logic without knowledge of social and emotional cues or social regard. Now we know that most autism is very limiting and requires a triage of occupational staff support and therapy, while a diagnosis of

Asperger's (a low spectrum of autism) can get you a job as a research scientist or accountant.

For instance, the character Sheldon, on the television series, "The Big Bang Theory" is an example of Aspergers. Numbers and science dominate his biological wiring, yet he is unable to manage or interpret emotions. Hence, range of functioning is not simply a binary answer. There is a range of functioning along a continuum. Spectrum disorders are now more understood.

Think about Spectrum: ....

I favor the Spectrum because, often times, people will not meet full criterion for a diagnosis or have only one or two impaired aspects of the illness. I also like it because often people will not meet the TRADITIONAL presentation of the disorder. Meaning that there are similarities and differences about the disorder. For instance with Autism, there is little to no eye contact made. However, with Asperger's disorder (a lower spectrum of Autism), eye contact may be brief or modeled, but can be made. These are two very different disorders, but they do have a minimal overlap in presentation.

The mental health field is like medicine; data shifts, discovery shifts, and it is fluid. It takes years to organize the statistics and research to get published. However, as knowledge changes and is incorporated, advances are made in treatment. This has been especially true for Bipolar disorder, and Bipolar spectrum.

Most people who are on the Bipolar spectrum don't have the obvious look of Bipolar I (with periods/days of highs with extreme energy, followed by days of lows with no energy.) For example, Bipolar II disorder is grossly misunderstood, and often missed entirely in diagnosis.

Bipolar II is almost identical to depression. Most doctors diagnose it and treat it as depression. The doctors need to be aware of the subtleties between the two to tell them apart. Most professionals don't know the subtleties between the two because of the way the research is written. Unless you spend hours and hours with these persons, it is very hard to discern a very mild mood elevation. The person just looks a bit more active and more socially at ease. They aren't hanging off of bar stools. So, it is very subtle. If the provider can find a better way to describe or ask the question, the person may be better able to identify that state themselves. So, when it comes to reporting symptoms, the mood shift to mood elevation is so slight it usually is overlooked or passed off as a "good day." However, there are subtle differences between Major Depressive Disorder and Bipolar II. The biggest issue being the way you treat it. The reality is that depression has one form of treatment and Bipolar II generally has a different combination of treatment. If you treat Bipolar II, as MDD, it may work for a period of time, but generally in the big picture, the person does not get better. The person can spend years doing therapy, but if the medication isn't right, then ultimately there is limited improvement.

Meet Bipolar II: Isn't all yellow, yellow?

What is Bipolar II? Bipolar II is described pretty much the same as Major Depression. No energy, no motivation, sad mood, and tearfulness. The negative mood state can vary from moderate to severe. Often, in the severe range a person can experience suicidal thinking that repeats over and over in their head. However, in between the depression, there are also episodes of "feeling normal." This is usually defined as having a better mood or brighter outlook, and ability to engage in regular household or job duties. People report cleaning and organizing shelves where normally they don't have the energy to do that. They catch up on the four loads of laundry that may be lurking in the hallway for the past week. Basically, it's an opportunity where things appear more "normal." Unfortunately, the energy level is brief and the positive mood doesn't last. My clients report it lasting may be two days maximum, but often it can last only a few hours. They then return to some level of "shifting" from normal mood to mid grade to severe depression. Depression is the most significant aspect of the disorder. What most people see is the depression. The energy shift is generally is so minimal that it usually is only noticed by the individual person. Naming different types of Bipolar has only created a lot more confusion. I believe a better name for Bipolar II disorder is "mood shifting depression," from moderate to severe. Mild depression is normal baseline and pretty much undetectable. Clients rarely would even notice it, and neither will the people around them because it's more like position neutral on the car. Even if you have Bipolar I, Bipolar II, or any spectrum mood, it has "good" mood in between these subtle shifts. The term Bipolar confuses people. This includes the professionals, because there are many shades to the disorder. It's like describing a color palette of yellow. Go to Sherwin Williams and tell them you want yellow paint. Imagine how they will look at you. Saying the room is yellow, gives you a generic idea because there are many shades of the same color; such as pale yellow, canary yellow, or sunset yellow. If you don't know what the shades look like, then you will buy the wrong color.

If you don't get the descriptor right; the treatment is far less effective, and a person's interest in treatment gets reduced. Why? Because at the end of the day, you were led to the wrong paint, since you didn't understand how the subtle shades of the spectrum work.

Bipolar Spectrum:

What most people are not aware of is that many patients fall on the lower end of the Bipolar spectrum. You are probably a stone's throw from several persons with the undiagnosed condition. You may even be working with them. They can be very high functioning. They will not present with distinctive periods of extreme highs followed by periods of extreme lows. Often Bipolar spectrum is very misconstrued. Doctors tend to use basic and overly simplistic factors to describe Bipolar, yet many persons do not fall under criteria such as spending large amounts of money and having a ravenous sex life. There are plenty of persons on the lower skew that this does not apply to. They have energy shifts, not compulsive sex addiction. I am not saying that this never occurs, it just seems to fall short in diagnosing many people who have mood and energy shifts that are more SUBTLE. It is true when people get in a higher mood state (elevated), they may be more prone to spending more money, gambling more, shopping more, and having more sex. You can almost say the same thing about people who are drunk. They generally do the same things. Professionals are getting lost in descriptive BEHAVIOR patterns with Bipolar, when it's more important to track ENERGY shifts and mood shifts.

I believe the key is not the behavior—those are signs. Those signs can also be overlapped with people who have personality problems (an entirely different style of behavioral and interpersonal difficulties). I believe the differences are in "energy" shifts from the barely subtle, to the mildly hyper, to the most obvious—irritable, argumentative, road rage, to fist fight. The Diagnostic manuals have not been able to strictly identify the subtle energy shifts as a significant paradigm. I believe that this is an error. Behavior is PART of the equation, but energy with mood state tells more of the story.

There is the multifactorial equation. For example, if you look at a person who becomes a stripper for a living. The behavior is stripping for income. Some would hypothesize that a person who does that likes sex, yet many people might say the total opposite. While others might say it's a job used to obtain money to avoid poverty. From economic survival to sexual promiscuity, for every hypothesis there is the possibility that it is entirely wrong. The behavior is still the same. So is the error rate. Therefore, I never use the behavior itself to come up with a hypothesis.

Where's the problem?

The real problem is lack of biological knowledge followed by lack of proper diagnosis. How do you treat something effectively, if the client can't describe it to you as a provider, or if as a provider you have a limited understanding of the spectrum of a disorder. Usually too, clients don't show up for their appointments on bad days, which is when they need to be seen most. Most clients need to be seen when they are moody or hyper or miserable, which often times does not happen. Most people do not understand mood disorders as biological markers, similar to a blood sugar level or blood pressure marker. The brain is an electrical grid that follows "code" to establish LEVELS for mood, metabolism, the ability to sense pain, and communication to coordinate a fight or flight response. All of these complex patterns fall under neurology or brain science.

Bad Descriptors:

Instead we as a society use poor descriptors to identify what is happening. "Oh, she's just moody as hell" Or "she has bad mood swings." I hate the term mood swings, because it is overused, may not take into account the underlying bad situation, and is often used in a derogatory manner. If you can't describe the mood swing as it happens, then it is likely the term is being used improperly. She has mood swings is about as clear as saying she likes vegetables. It's very vague. Yet, people interviewing will ask the question with good intent. It's just a lousy question. The other term that is used in research, that I find only messes up a diagnosis is grandiosity. "Grandiosity" is supposed to be a feeling of entitlement, self-righteousness, and even higher arrogance. People with mood disorders RARELY ever feel that way, UNLESS they are completely drunk or completely manic.

What does manic mean?

Manic is just supercharged energy, but at its extreme, it can get grandiose/super self-absorbed. People who are not happy manic tend to be pissed off manic, which is extremely angry. So, it refers to high volume energy with either good mood or anger. Now back to the term of grandiosity above. In my clinical work most people did not deliver as "grandiose," and the question usually misleads.

Manic (Hyper) people are so comfortable in their skin, with their energy, and sometimes irritability, and they are able to tell you where to go and how to get there. Persons with depression or anxiety rarely feel great. So, I think using the term grandiosity in research does not deliver effectively. The term grandiosity describes full blown mania and should have nothing to do with a Bipolar II diagnosis. In Bipolar II, there is smaller energy spurt instead of mania and that is called hypomania. Hypo means under. "Hypomania" most likely presents as a good mood with some energy and sociability behind it.

Researchers use words for descriptors, but that doesn't always deliver properly. Clinicians have to deal with it live, so they get a different presentation. That's like comparing the chemist who comes up with treatments for making healthy grass to the lawn guy who has seen and treated 800 lawns.

The two don't always agree. There is theory on what is supposed to happen, but that doesn't mean it plays out exactly as it is conceptualized.

Mood disorders can be better defined as depression, anxiety or Bipolar. Essentially, in my work clients who have depression, usually have the anxiety too. As depression gets more severe, anxiety and self-consciousness kicks in. The other term I use is the PPP (The Personal Paranoia Program). What this means is a person gets hyper-anxious and isolates themselves from others because of self-consciousness issues that can look like paranoia, but the person is not really globally paranoid. For instance, a person who abuses substances and starts to believe that squirrels are talking about him, this is not what I am referring to. Whether something is just a straight shot Unipolar (1 sided condition), which is a zero energy depression or anxiety, instead of a manic quality anxiety, or whether it has a spectrum look to it, really requires some good information from providers who understand the full range of Bipolar spectrum NOT professionals who refer to the generic term of Bipolar .

Why? Because historically, the only way people have ever understood Bipolar is using one or two parameters to describe great highs followed by great lows. If that's the way they measure it, then they are missing many people who are under the "softer" end of the spectrum. A great reference for this is the book, *Why am I still Depressed?* by Jim Phelps, MD. Most people don't have the high/low extreme presentation. So, you should be talking to a Provider who understands the full spectrum of it rather than a general high/low principle. The high/

low principle has the metaphorical equivalent of all or nothing problem-solving, which does not work. Don't problem solve with a person who only has one working model.

When You Start to Question How You Feel...

I have seen several hundreds of Bipolar clients, from the spectrum on up, and find that the biggest problem is that they don't know they have the disorder. They think they have anxiety, when it's more like a manic level of anxiety. They think it's a depression, when the depression is actually a mood-shifting depression from say moderate with low motivation, to severe where they don't or can't get out of bed and start to get suicidal thoughts. There seems to be a relatively constant shift that is uncomfortable, alternating with spaces where they feel good. The brain moves up chemicals and then drops them off, sometimes erratically. The person also has periods where they feel completely fine. The drop offs are very hard to see or explain. They drop off like blood sugar would. You don't see it, but you feel it. Unfortunately, these same people will take an antidepressant or two that don't seem to work. They don't work, because the chemical equation requires a different combination.

For example, when you ramp up too high, you will get an uncomfortable level of energy. We call these people busy bees. Nope. They just have an overdose of norepinephrine in their brain, that keeps them moving hard and long. Some of these people will start exercising excessively in the name of good health. It isn't so much about good health as it is burning off an excess of energy. Depending on how manic you get—I just use the word hyper to understand it better—you may start on different projects, but not really be effective in finishing anything. Why? Because the energy is there, but the concentration checked out a long time ago. Sitting still and reading is a no-can-do, because the person is so revved up that you cannot focus, and you have to move around to feel more comfortable. If you can't focus, then you can't complete anything. The person just usually thinks it's just depression, anxiety, or OCD. For the record, in my clinical career, I have never met a person who had Obsessive Compulsive Disorder in isolation. This being said, I've always seen it co-occur with a Bipolar condition. OCD, in my clinical opinion, is not a stand alone condition; despite what most people think. If you are treating it independently and notice it isn't getting much better, considering checking for mood changes, and if they are making your OCD worse.

So there's the rev-up and there's a rev down. The problem is seeing the milder shifts. The milder shifts can present as irritability or crankiness. Their friend or partner might say, "what's wrong? You seem like something is bothering you?" The person usually responds, "I'm fine," but their response style and their shift is noticeable to someone close to them. It usually escapes the client's attention. Those are mild shifts, but they are shifts. If a person starts wanting to argue more, there's a strong possibility this is happening. The client who is inexperienced in recognizing a mood shift, may start attributing it to some outside circumstance or person that they now find annoying. Sometimes the client fails to recognize their neurotransmitters have faltered, creating a sense of internal discomfort that is going to be picked up on by others.

Spectrum persons can have some mild mood elevation. What that means is that they have an elevation (a little higher) compared to their own baseline, which is normally low. They feel good enough to start clearing off loads of laundry that have been sitting, cleaning out dishes in the sink, or starting to clean up the masses of stacked clothes in the bedroom. They may even feel "good" enough to go shopping. However, this mood state does not last long, sometimes just a few hours. My clients generally experience it for a maximum of two days, at most, and then it goes back to some degree of low energy and depression.

The problem with this scenario, is that most Providers will not understand this as part of the spectrum (because the researchers who provide data questionnaires often times superimpose hypomania with mania, which will confuse and misdiagnose the Bipolar II persons.) In Jim Phelps, MD; "Why Am I Still Depressed?," he uses the BSDS (Bipolar Spectrum Diagnostic Scale) developed by Ron Pies, MD. The BSDS is golden in my experience.

Trouble spots equally occur because the client, when they go to see their doctor, have a hard time describing their mood or energy or any form of changes. So most of the time, if a client is struggling, then they may not even show up for their appointment because they feel bad, and the therapist does not get an opportunity to see what is happening. Because of this incomplete information, the client is likely just treated with an antidepressant that starts to work, but then stops, as well as something like Xanax to slow down their agitated energy. This little "miscommunication" cycle can go on for years. The problem with that is that the therapy struggles to keep the person going from situation to situation, when in fact, it is similar to trying to balance mood between blood sugar spikes and drops, and wonder why the person has a hard time staying glued.

Chemical Shifts:

If you want to understand what a chemical shift looks like, go talk to a night owl. Talk to them at night and then talk to them in the morning. Now, do the same for early risers. Early risers only get up well in the morning; if you talk to them at night, they are zombies. The exact opposite occurs with night owls. Night owls are fabulous at night, but horrific in the morning. These people have a miserable time waking up in the morning, but at night, they can get most things done. Why? Because neurotransmitters that provide energy, concentration, and motivation show up for night owls in the early evening, instead of the morning. The exact opposite is true for early risers. This disrupts the person's ability to fall asleep. In the early morning, night owls sleep hardest, and they are the walking dead if you try to move them. They blow through several alarms, and might be late for work, if you don't wrestle them out of their early morning coma. It really is not a matter of them having bad sleep hygiene, as much as it is an issue with biochemistry and circadian rhythm (genetic body rhythms) shifts that wake them up in the latter part of the day. Can this be manipulated or improved? In short, yes. In my clinical experience, most persons with Bipolar or Bipolar spectrum are not psychotic.

Psychotic meaning having false beliefs that are bizarre; such as the CIA is putting a bugging device in their food. These are delusions. Psychosis can also occur with having visual or auditory hallucinations. At the end of the day, Bipolar or the spectrum just requires some working knowledge of how mood chemicals in the brain are shifting to create uncomfortable symptoms, and different ways to make them stick in a more effective pattern. The biggest problem is that incomplete information results in bad treatment options.

The term Bipolar is very misunderstood and misused, so I think people on the spectrum should fall under a different heading. Before the field understood Asperger's disorder, people fell under the heading of Autism, which was very inaccurate. Mood disorders, and their hybrids or spectrum, require different medications, supplements, diet, and lifestyle changes to assist.

Not all mood symptoms fall under Bipolar, and yet some fall under the spectrum. It is because mood disorders are triggered by physical changes regulated and triggered by mood chemicals (neurotransmitters). Diabetics have to regulate and manipulate the use of insulin to be able to function more effectively. With mood disorders, such as depression, anxiety, or Bipolar, the abundance or absence of mood chemicals in the brain (serotonin, norepinephrine, dopamine)can trigger good or bad moods as well as physical symptoms. The person may or may not opt to use medication. But it is critical to have a good ability to describe energy changes, thought changes, motivation, and sleep changes, so that the professionals can evaluate better medications and interventions. Tracking your sleep is a useful descriptor—do you get insomnia? Do you wake up frequently? Do you have periods where you cannot sleep? Do you get tightness in your chest? Does your heart race? Do you get a pit in your stomach? Do you look at food and feel like you can't eat? Do you binge eat? Do you have nervous thoughts? Do you get one thought that chases another? Is it hard to sort your thoughts? Do you have to keep moving? Are you constantly distracted? Do you have a hard time concentrating? Is your memory shot? Do you get frequent problems with anger? Do you get tickets? Do you have to take naps during the day? Do you have dragging energy?

Are you a morning person? Are you an evening person? Do you hate change? Do you look forward to change? What type of work interests do you have? Is it easy for you to come up with ideas? Are you generally accurate about the amount of money that you spend in a week? Do you pay your bills on time? Are you linear or abstract in your thinking?

These are just a few types of questions that I find more helpful than what the traditional guidelines provide. And no, it's not in the research, but it has worked in my practice. Although I am an advocate of scientific research, I won't use that as my sole measure because of the potential for research/researcher error, sampling, and design problems. At the end of the day, the house is only constructed with the integrated expertise of the homeowner, architect, and design engineer (and their level of experience). If what we go with is just what the homeowner desires, there may be a problem with functionality and engineering.

Hello Biology:

Sleep, appetite, and mood functions are on the same biological curve. Get one, it can start off slow, but eventually becomes a domino effect across all. Most people don't notice these smaller things. Loss of appetite or increased appetite isn't generally on someone's radar, unless they have significant weight changes to show for it. You can have a lot of weight loss, and people will still error on the side that it is a healthy thing. They run in multiple marathons, keep a pedometer on at all times, and insist that this is health at its finest. Wrong. People who have high degrees of agitation have very low Body Mass Index and also tend to walk or exercise any weight off their body. They perceive it as healthy. What they don't say is that it creates a relief in their body from agitation. What's worse is that society and doctors even offer congratulations (unless you cross into the visibly ill or the Anorexic pole). These signs are easily overlooked or misunderstood even by the people who do them.

Instead when people don't feel well (irritable, depressed, angry) they are more likely to look at their date of the night, sex partner, or lack of an intimate partner as the problem, or their work life as the problem, or their finances as the stressor. These may be irritants and stressors, but there can be underlying mechanisms causing stress on your brain that push you past your limit. Unless you study neuroscience, you would not know that the brain chemicals and receptors sites are not doing their job.

Don't Steep or Drop:

With depression or mood disorders, the brain struggles to regulate multiple mood brain chemicals (such as serotonin, norepinephrine, and dopamine) to foster healthy emotional stability. By stability, I mean operating with a functional mood and energy level. Not getting too low or steeping too high. Essentially, problems with sleep, appetite, concentration, and mood disturbances describe clinical depression. Unknowledgeable persons might say, "he's got to stop feeling sorry for himself and just think positive." To make matters worse from already looking like a weakling, people who are depressed, may become increasingly tearful because of the stress on the body. It is usually a mistake to assume that someone wants to cry to get your attention.

People have been so wrong for generations. They may be judgmental, because they don't understand how the body works. Once these chemical levels are treated in the body, then sleep starts to become more regulated. No more insomnia. Stops the crying. No more fitful sleep with constantly waking up. You can do all the sleep hygiene you want by going to bed at a certain time and waking up at the same time or lowering your activity by bed time. That doesn't mean anything if you have a mood disorder. A mood disorder will curse your sleep, which will lead you to alternate between sleep deprivation and oversleeping on a regular basis. And as you treat one part, it will be easier to improve the others.

A mood disorder is discernible by multiple changes in the body. Blood sugar problems are also discernible by multiple changes in the body too (most would agree). You can have blood sugar levels that are too high or too low and no-one is going to tell you to get yourself out of it. Biological screw-ups are physiological. They do create psychological distress. You will get distressed when you can't concentrate to make a simple decision, have no energy to bathe, live on a few crackers and cheese, but you will think it's because of X or Y. The levels are connected. On the cellular level, your brain is an electrical motherboard. The motherboard regulates all other functions and communications in the body. If there is no communication or impaired levels that regulate a specific function such as attention, the function will be negatively impacted. The motherboard is also pre-loaded with viruses. These viruses are genetic. They will play out, and continue to play out, until the motherboard is able to de-activate the switch that turns on the virus and re-regulate the levels to where they need to be.

For example, the *National Institute of Health* wrote an article (Sept. of 2012), about the link between the Gata 1 gene and depression. The article is called, "The Genetic Switch Involved in Depression." The article shows an image of brain mapping, and the cell communication in a control brain versus the cell communication of a person with depression (Gata 1 active). The control brain looks like a busy, well lit, interstate road flowing in all directions. However, the brain with depression (when the gene is active) shows a dimly lit road, with half the road with road blocks or traffic shut-down. This is why the person who is experiencing depression or Bipolar suffers. Those roads represent various levels of functioning in the body. If they shut down, then the person will feel miserable.

The brain keeps trying to find alternate highways to fill-in for the shut-down; the same way you look for an alternate route when traffic is jammed on the freeway. So, to anyone who was told, "You just need to get a grip," you need to respond with some intelligence on the matter. There's biological functions that get messed up with mood disorders. It's very much treatable, but you have to understand where to look. Most people don't know where to look. In other words, you need to educate. Genetic codes get hampered under stress and often under-fire or misfire. That causes chemical changes that cause psychological changes in functioning and a host of different ways to feel absolutely miserable. .

Bipolar disorder is a condition where brain chemicals shift away from a normative baseline (similar to the way blood sugar levels might). When serotonin is higher, it provides happiness, good will, and good thoughts. The world is a noble place. When serotonin is lower, the person feels depressed, anxious, and lousy. For example, how many times have you had to attend a wedding that you did not want to? You look around at the assigned seating with dread, and wonder who you are forced to engage in social conversation with? Every party has a mouthpiece, a "no filter," or what I call the alcohol messenger. If you have a line of people that are broke, the messenger will send the word "cash" bar via hand signals (for those who don't want to be known as cheap). Either broke or not broke, the infamous word is "bar." The bartender becomes the rescue squad to a weary and socially awkward wedding party. And when the booze is flowing, so do the positive thoughts and chummy relationships—at least for a few hours.

Alcohol In The Picture:

Once we have that drink of wine or beer, our brain no longer cares about our social discomfort. We are willing to tolerate others better and are less self-conscious. Our thoughts and words generally are more positive, at least for a while. But, it's not an if, it's a when. Eventually, the serotonin in the brain comes to a halt and the receptor sites are used up. At that point, our mood starts to take a nosedive. For some people, it's the next day. For others, with significant mood swings or alcohol problems, if the serotonin falls off too steep, the irritability enters, and so do the fights. Bad thoughts replace good thoughts. When the serotonin level DROPS, it provides the opposite—irritability, depression, negative, and sad thinking. People can even get beyond sentimental. They get tearful. The problem is that alcohol ultimately acts as a depressant. It muses as charm, but will ultimately rob you of calm. This is why bad domestic fights can erupt when a lot of alcohol has been flowing.

Serotonin imbalances can also been seen with persons who struggle with Obsessive Compulsive Disorder. The person cannot feel calm until all the dishes are washed out of the sink, (no matter how late the party), compulsive rituals in bathing (taking multiple baths per day), or other cleanliness rituals— the cabinets have alphabetic organization, the furnishings not only have placement in the house, but the person can tell if the picture frame has been moved within a matter of three degrees. When others move things around without the same level of exactness, the person becomes irritable and difficult. When the serotonin is lacking, the brain feels overwhelmed and the person becomes driven by obsessive thinking and compulsive behavior.

People with Bipolar Can Function:

The stereotype is that Bipolar people don't function. This is untrue. Do they suffer with some aspect of managing mood symptoms? Yes. Does this make them non-functional across all spheres? No. In contrast, there are many high functioning persons with spectrum Bipolar who have executive level jobs. They can be extremely successful monetarily as well as within their profession. So whatever you think you know about the illness; think again.

For example, there have been celebrities/musicians/artists who are enormously talented, and have come forth to say that they have battled depression or Bipolar symptoms. Bruce Springsteen, Mariah Carey, Katy Perry, Niki Minaj, Demi Lovato, and Catherine Zeta-Jones. People who have the ability to say that this is not only treatable, but a person can also be successful. One of our favored Presidents, Abraham Lincoln, spent most of his life severely depressed, yet he was considered one of the best president we ever had. The UK had the great Winston Churchill, who had "Manic Depression", currently called Bipolar I. And so on…If Major Depression or Bipolar spectrum was the path to destruction, then how is it that we recognize these people as successful?

Recognition for Bipolar spectrum is still lagging behind for several reasons including lack of good information and faulty assumptions. The main assumption is that these people may not be successful. Wrong. Many are. However, the people who acknowledge the disorder, and treat it effectively, can and do get better. The untreated are in a class by themselves. They do have the worst outcomes.

For one, people are afraid of the stigma of having what is currently labeled as a mental illness. So, many take a strong defense against effective treatment. Often it may take many years before a person is willing to recognize mood spectrum and treat it effectively. For example, people who are programmed for perfection will likely spend more years not getting treated effectively. Nobody wants to be seen as different. Now look at those people down the road—usually they are miserable. Be courageous and do what you need to do. Bring some progress into a situation.

Family Judgment or Neglect:

Parents or family that is judgmental never helped anyone. If anything, your judgment has delayed helping that person. For those of you who have no regard for medications or counseling, you may be inadvertently or directly stopping the person who is close to you from reaching out for better treatment. If you are that person, you need to reconsider your position—many lives depend on it. Unfortunately, I've seen too many sorry souls, who gave their family member a hard time about this type of treatment and were left with a pile of regret and guilt.

Mood disorders are a genetic condition (they are physiological, which means of the body). It affects the mind, AND it wreaks havoc on the body. The mind and the body are connected. The mind makes interpretations based upon the physical signals that the brain sends and receives. What if one of the most widely misunderstood psychological disorders is largely comprised of changes that are physical? Should we still call it a mental illness? Do we refer to people with blood sugar problems as having a mental disorder? Because the blood sugar changes can cause mood swings and can effect their mental health. Low blood sugar can cause brain fog and cognitive deficits. Mental health is helpful to point out where the symptoms are present (thinking, concentration, decision-making, mood). However, as an overall treatment strategy, it is limited. Diabetics need to rely on insulin to regulate their blood sugar levels because levels can vacillate widely out of range. Should you view yourself poorly because you have blood pressure problems? The point I am trying to make is that the term "mental" appears more accurately to be termed medical, and mental health historically stopped generations of people from getting the help they needed regulating and treating the origins of often a stress-induced, chemical, and genetic equation.

People with the spectrum tend to experience mood symptoms, but they don't necessarily think it is part of the Bipolar spectrum. Often times it is mistaken for depression, severe anxiety, or any other subtype of anxiety. The symptoms look like low energy or low motivation with interrupted sleep patterns or insomnia. They can also get obsessive thought patterns. Obsessive thoughts can be better described as thoughts that are negative and repetitive in their own nature. (In contrast, when people hear the word obsessive, they often think of Obsessive Compulsive Disorder, which ties thoughts into behaviors such as compulsive hand washing, people who are germophobes, or people who have to have relentless organization in their drawers and cabinets). This is different from obsessive thoughts. Obsessive thoughts keep circling in a different way from OCD, yet they are equally very distressing. When a person gets severely depressed and has obsessive thoughts of self-harming and suicide become predominant.

With the spectrum, there can be social anxiety—where one minute a person can be very sociable and the next where they don't want to leave the house. The person is so physically uncomfortable that they cannot tolerate being around others. Yet at other times (when the mood improves) they can appear sociable. This becomes very confusing to witness and equally upsetting for the person who experiences it. It appears to be a conspiracy of opposites.

Bipolar and Transportation:

In the Bipolar spectrum brain, mood chemicals will rev up or drop off erratically. The patient may experience energy surges that are positive, as in "I get a lot of stuff done." They can organize, clean, shop, and paint to the point of wearing others out. Or they can get the down side consisting of lower energy, sad mood, anger, or tearfulness. In this space, it takes nearly all of their energy just to do basic things such as bathing. You may be shocked at the amount of dishes in the sink. Tasks that require great energy or concentration will be avoided. The physiology of the body in the spectrum has neural connections that do not communicate effectively. The equivalent is having a cab show up at the right time at the wrong address. You want to get somewhere, but you are stalled out because the GPS is defunct or temporarily out of service. Sometimes you can get there. Other times, the system isn't working, and the result is completely inconsistent behavior . This makes the person very hard to rely on. People want to make a mood disorder, a personal character problem, when it is in fact, a medical problem with biochemistry levels and communication distress that presents with MULTIPLE body challenges.

CHARACTERISTICS OF MOOD DISORDERS:

SLEEP PROBLEMS:

Do you find that the minute you go to lie down, your brain is non-stop and hyper alert with one thought chasing another? If you are willing to get out of bed, you could write down some of your ideas. They could work. You have a lot of energy at the wrong time. You could probably start your day when it should be ending. Some of your best problem-solving happens when most people are asleep. It is very frustrating because you end up going to work exhausted like the walking dead.

According to the article, "Good Night and Good Luck: Norepinephrine in Sleep Pharmacology" Mitchell, H.A. et al. . *Biochem Pharmacology* 2010, NCBI-NIH, sleep involves complex interactions "between multiple brain regions and neuromodulators." Norepinephrine, "NE long known for its role in maintaining general arousal, is also a crucial player in sleep pharmacology." The neurotransmitter norepinephrine (NE), impacts the efficacy of many wake-and sleep-promoting medications." "NE also influences the synthesis of Melatonin."

Forbes "These neurotransmitters are probably keeping you up at night" *Quora*, (October 5, 2016) Gerber, Colin; Neuroscientist.

"Norepinephrine activity in the locus coeruleus (LC) is the most important with regards to the sleep-wake cycle. This is one of the main areas involved in arousal from sleep. Increased norepinephrine also decreases REM sleep." This article also discusses the role of GABA, as a neurotransmitter that helps shut things down or inhibits response. It states that increasing GABA "contributes to inducing sleep."

According to the article by sleep doctor, Michael J. Breus PhD, DABSM "How to sleep better Understanding GABA," GABA is responsible for calming the activity of the brain, and includes "increased relaxation, reduced stress, a more calm, balanced mood alleviation of pain, and a boost to sleep." "A number of natural supplements affect GABA activity, to help relieve stress and anxiety."

"GABA-ergic sleep-promoting medications like benzodiazepines and benzodiazepine-like drugs that act more specifically on benzodiazepine receptors increase the activity of GABA, which inhibits NE transmission". Mitchell H. A. et al. *Biochem Pharmacology* 2010.

When people ask their parents how they slept as a child, they may say "you were impossible to put down for a nap." Believe it or not, these behaviors appear relatively stable despite age. Stable meaning that the chemical equation that was erratic and produced sleep deficiency as a child will persist into adulthood. The brain turns on the "alert" button with rises in norepinephrine (energy), when it should be building GABA (calming, sedating). There is a very real answer to why sleep is problematic. There are multiples of neurotransmitters, hormones, and neuro-pathways involved in alertness (arousal) and sleep regulation, as well as multiple neurological pathways involved in sleep disorders as evidenced above. Those are the tip of the iceberg to provide a general overview. Both the system/pathway and the neurotransmitter messengers must function well to provide adequate sleep. Head injury such as a stroke or brain damage to the pathways can result in sleep disorder. Mood disorder can also contribute to sleep disorder.

There is a chemical equation in your brain that involves location, receptor firing, which is similar to dialing something up versus dialing something down on a receptor, as well as what the chemical or hormonal messengers are, and how they can influence. Whether the role is an agonist, "which acts like another substance and stimulates an action" Antagonist is the opposite. *Medicine Net,* Shiel, William J. Jr. MD, FACP, FACR. "An agonist is a chemical that binds to a receptor and activates the receptor to produce a biological response. "An antagonist blocks the action of the agonist". *Wikipedia.* There are many people who regularly have sleep problems and take some type of sleep aid such as Benadryl or Ambien. Assuming that the person does not have some type of brain damage or does not suffer from Narcolepsy or Sleep Apnea, it may be likely that a MOOD disorder is causing the sleep problem. So, if sleep is a chronic problem, a mood disorder caused by offset neurotransmitter challenges is worth taking a closer look at.

APPETITE CHANGES:

With mood disorders, another notable biological change is loss of appetite. People experiencing depression and anxiety may be prone to lose weight. They may be misperceived as having an eating disorder. It may look like one, but the origin is completely different. The person is not trying to lose weight, count calories, binge, or purge. Persons with depression or anxiety don't necessarily have body dysmorphic disorder, which is a gateway for eating disorders. In contrast, for instance, a person with severe anxiety often loses their appetite or feels sick to their stomach when they eat. As a result, they start to lose weight. The same symptoms appear for a people who suffer from depression. It is a SECONDARY effect, rather than a primary motivator with an eating disorder.

With mood disorders, it is NOT uncommon to lose biological hunger cues. Weight loss is a by-product of neurological and chemical underpinnings. In my practice, I have noted that younger people tend to lose more weight versus older persons who generally tend to have increased appetite and weight gain. As people age, metabolic shifts may take precedence in which direction will predominate. Younger people generally do not have metabolic syndrome and insulin resistance, and tend towards the weight loss. Exceptions do apply.

CONCENTRATION PROBLEMS:

Mood disorders cause disruptions in the ability to concentrate. A person will start noticing that it takes them a lot longer to finish their work that normally they could finish fairly quickly. A long term concentration problem, that is noted in the early years, is usually identified as a form of Attention Deficit Disorder.

Mood disorders can give you concentration problems that are almost identical to Attention Deficit Disorder but are not rooted there. Focus and decision-making can be so difficult. Clients would say a decision as simple as what to wear in the morning would be overwhelming.

Many believe the concentration problems look so similar to Attention Deficit Disorder, that they must have late-onset ADHD. It is true, there are some confusing and overlapping symptoms between ADHD and Bipolar. Many people are not treated for the mood symptoms, and it takes several years before a person who is Bipolar or on the Bipolar spectrum gets accurately diagnosed. This is often because of self-reporting problems, not providing family history problems, years of multiple trials of ineffective medications , and because depression has a mirror twin of Bipolar II. These errors often co-mingle with , Provider lack of knowledge of spectrum type moods. More people with untreated Bipolar spectrum are taking treatments for ADHD, for concentration problems, and low energy problems, yet they are not getting any better. The reason they are not getting better is that the source of the concentration problems are rooted in neurotransmitter changes consistent with mood disorders.

Same Symptom different Cause:

In my experience, when the patients who do not respond to the ADHD meds are switched to antidepressant or mood stabilizers, the concentration and energy problems improve. So, it may look like ADHD, but it doesn't necessarily need to be treated with ADHD meds. For instance, if you have a common cold, you may have sinus drainage that starts a cough. You can also have a cough from Pneumonia. If you treat the Pneumonia with the standard antibiotic, the person will likely not get better. Pneumonia's cough requires a different treatment. This is the way I tend to view the ADHD versus mood disorder- based concentration problem. Same symptom, different origin. Different origin requires different medication.

The science behind medicine and psychology are fluid. We are still learning and differentiating diagnosis. For example, years ago treating someone with panic disorder was about explaining what anxiety is and also doing some breath work and progressive relaxation strategies. If the anxiety is mild, these methods can be introduced and likely get a modicum of improvement. However, if you have ever witnessed a person having a full blown panic attack, in the midst of it, breath work can be a little late with poor outcome. Like trying to stop a train.

In the movie, "Sully" Tom Hanks' character was being discredited because he bypassed many of the "standard" flying procedures that would be in play to avoid a crash. The character had to take his knowledge and condense it into a few steps. Life is different from research, theory, and speculation. Medical health/mental health is not one size fits all. What works in an acute crisis may be significantly different than a mild situation. Keeping in mind the origin of anxiety can have a different presentation; ranging from a situational induced anxiety to a severe anxious mania with a strong biochemical basis often seen in Bipolar. The quantity and quality of agitation and impact differ significantly.

An important factor to understand is that moods are heavily biologically driven. Mood is NOT the personality. People assume that it is personality. Untrue. It is a descriptor that should not be used to define personality.

Personality disorders are about the Psychology behind impaired or destructive personality styles.

Personality disorders create a large amount of distress for people who have to deal with these personalities. Personality disorders are a style of interacting. They can be learned. They are not chemically caused. Unfortunately, they are rampant. Narcissistic Personality Disorder, Borderline Personality Disorder, Antisocial Personality Disorder to name the big ones. These are just some of the more common styles we see.

Most people don't have a working knowledge of what a personality disturbance is. It is a way of interpreting and responding to the world that becomes rather fixed in it's approach. Meaning very limited in the likelihood of changing it. People with Personality disorders want others to change, not themselves. Personality disorders are not necessarily triggered by mood chemicals, they are triggered by a person's beliefs, their abusive or maladaptive early backgrounds, how they want things done, who they may want to manipulate, or how they want to be seen.

Personality disorders are a restrictive style of interacting with people. This is the stuff that people complain about in other people. For example, "I spent my life married to a narcissist." "He's a sociopath." "She's a control freak." "She can't make a decision without interviewing ten people." These are not mood problems. These are personality patterns that people like to engage that irritate others around them. This is how they manipulate or interact with people around them. These behavioral issues always serve a purpose around their personality. For instance, control freaks yell and scream because they want everyone to do exactly what they want to avoid any form of change. Change is intolerable to them. So, they fight back with increasingly aversive counter measures. When people say they have been married to a narcissist, try and substitute the words with a socially charming and self-serving personality style.

It is possible that personality disorders can co-occur with a mood disorder. However, many people with mood disorders do NOT have Personality disorders.

Bad labels aren't necessarily about mood...they can be personality:

Personality disorders are a problem. Some of the false labeling of people comes from confusing a mood disorder with a personality disorder. Personality disorder is a chosen style of interacting with others but the mood disorder is not.

Mood disorders carry severe internal distress. Personality disordered persons usually cause distress on others. It is possible to have both. However, much of what people complain about in people are Personality disorders, rather than mood disorders.

People with mood disorders are sensitive. The term that is overused today is "empath," which is short for empathic. An empath, from my experience base, is usually seeking some type of identification. People with a sensitive nature that is naturally endowed, don't try to highlight it. If anything, they would rather downplay it. Although most people with mood disorders don't like to bring attention to themselves, many are quite intuitive and read social cues easily. They often attune to other's needs better than their own. They tend to withdraw, isolate , or experience anxiety. This is not a character trait problem. It only becomes a character trait problem IF a personality disorder is attached.

Personality Disorders are Free Agents:

Personality disorders are free floating disorders—a free agent so to speak. They can exist by themselves without the presence of a mood condition. The personality problems can cause extreme distress for persons around them. However, more difficult cases can have both a mood disturbance and a personality disturbance. This is often the case in Borderline personality.

Borderline personality disorder (BPD) presents when a person who is very sensitive (which is both positive and negative), has an erratic, inconsistent response style, and can be tough on others and even worse on themselves. Attachment history is usually very poor, which makes trust very difficult to obtain. There is a very reactive response style at the perceived or real threat of being abandoned or potentially taken advantage of. Emotional stress tends to be chronic, unless the person is actively involved in treatment. Unfortunately, these persons with the BPD personality style tend to assume the worst in others, and use that as a foundation.

BPD persons usually were victimized by emotional neglect, sexual or physical abuse, or other extreme trauma. The trauma stays active at the base. The problem is that under disagreement, may tend to color others with negative intent. Anger is the alpha and the omega and justifies everything terrible in between. It is a very painful emotional living space to navigate.

In the worst, but not all, of the BPD, false accusations are common. These persons have an unstable sense of self, vacillating between all importance, entitlement, to zeroing out at no self-worth. They can be spotted in the crowd as persons who are often very intelligent, tend towards splitting people in good or bad categories, or being a bit of a "stick-stirrer." Anger tends to be a big key. This lends to a high level of unpredictability. Many tend to be very generous. Most BPD, in my experience, have the backdrop of a Bipolar condition. What that means is that mood irritability and swings contribute negatively to the equation. In a good mood, you are idealized, and the "most" wonderful person they ever met. In a bad or depressed mood, you are a jerk who is only using them and deserve the wrath of hell.

Unfortunately, there is a history of some type of abuse or neglect instituted by persons close to them that propels this disorder into constant trauma states, and often self-harming states, which puts them at higher risk of suicide. If you recognize this in someone, by all means seek out Psychiatric consultation and therapy to assist.

The worst of the BPD personality types will deliberately blame others wrongly and enjoy bringing someone to personal ruin. Again, that is not everyone with this diagnosis. I believe a better way to label this may be a revenge-seeking personality. When the good part of the relationship is over, do they seek to discredit or attack you? Abandonment is a huge trigger. These persons may struggle with hate and like at the same time. One minute you are the best person in the world, but that can change rather quickly. They tend to cross contaminate their negative motives onto others. Maliciousness rises especially if they feel initially rejected. Generally, no problems will happen if they reject you first. If triggered badly, a severe BPD tends to manipulate and lie. They generally do not get involved in outward or visible illegal activities. They do not rob people of money, but they might rob them of their social standing. BPD is known for their personal and social attacks. The attack will usually be triggered by a perceived emotional loss. BPD's at their best are very socially attuned and care for everyone, including children and animals.

Grade A threats involve an emotional threat, as opposed to a financial threat by the other party, such as divorce custody, another lover, etc.

An example of a BPD was a woman on You Tube was beating herself physically and attempting to blame her husband for the abuse. Luckily for him, there was a camera that showed her beating herself. This person with BPD was clearly okay with self-harming behavior, which most people don't understand. Let's face it, if the camera wasn't in place, that man would have been wrongfully charged, and would have spent years in a jail cell. Years ago, I wonder how many people got wrongly convicted because of these behaviors?

The disclaimer is that not everyone with BPD is as extreme: I am speaking of the strongest clinical presentation. Keep in mind, a person may have features of BPD without showing all the symptoms.

BPD persons are very sane, intelligent, and not psychotic. Their super warmth or their super wrath can help people recognize them. Negative or exploitive relationship motives are often what they assume from others, which is a very painful space to draw from. The tendency is to blow up the relationship, rather than try to manage any form of healthy conflict or disagreement. This makes it hard for well intentioned persons. Unfortunately, mid ground is very hard to interpret for them. Many were exposed to abuse and they tend to operate in the extremes of behavior responses, and project onto others equally dark motives. It takes a very long time to earn their trust.

BPD attacks, often get a pass in court rooms and therapist's office, because they have painful histories. Professionals know this in advance, and tend to prefer to not work with them because of the potential for destructive and negative attacks if challenged in any way. The problem is that the professionals that generally do this work, do it without any form of challenge, and persons with BPD do not get better. The effectiveness, in my opinion, is therapy that has some challenge.

Some Psychological disorders such as BPD and Antisocial PD may require court-ordered or supervised therapy because of their tendency to discredit others if challenged. If persons with BPD are to get better, they need to assume accountability along with support for the people who do the work.

Narcissistic Personality:

This is one of the trendiest personality disorders to date. Simply put, persons with NPD are self-serving. They are not sociopath/antisocial or BPD. They are not interested in destroying your life. They are interested in emptying it. When you have not much to offer them, they are done with you. They are interested in looking good and having the best of everything. They are meticulously groomed. They should be called "best in show." They also appear charming and socially outgoing. Many times that is not who they really are internally. If they are interested in what you have, then they are interested in you. Whatever goods you are selling i.e. social connections, physical assets, family money, or titles. They are interested in power, money, and visibility. If you are a support to them, then they will want you with them. When they are with you, then they are really "on." You feel supported and attuned. However, deep attachment does not happen with these persons. That fault line had cracked a long time before you entered the picture. Often times it takes a narcissist to raise a narcissist. Long term partners believe they can show them warmth and affection. They become shocked and become emotionally dismantled when the partner realizes the lack of emotional generosity towards them. They may buy their partners nice gifts or offer great parties, but again, this is a mirror strategy that reflects back on them in a good way. Narcissists appear to offer up a simplified version of empathy for others, but it isn't one that you would like to call upon. They are good at looking socially concerned, but if it doesn't involve them, then they really don't offer much. NPD feeds on givers, meaning they seek out milder, giving personalities that provide support to them. Takers can sniff out another taker a mile away. You will not see two NPDs together. NPD is usually paired with a quieter, supportive person, who enjoys the gregariousness of the NPD. NPD is known to play cat and mouse with romantic interests. Once you are not interested, then they start calling you. They will pursue you until you pursue them. That isn't very stimulating for them. If you get too needy that is a turn off. A relationship with an NPD will continue as long as you have something to offer. NPDs get bored easily with life. They are constantly looking for new ways to entertain themselves as well as new people to do it with. They love the mind games of strategy and manipulation. They love visibility and achievement. They cannot tolerate being invisible. They make good parents because they will put in all the right structural supports for their children to succeed. They make poor parents because that doesn't usually involve much deep emotional support. The NPD usually leads where their priorities are first. Unfortunately, emotional connections are secondary to achievement and visibility. This is not uncommon with people who have high profile careers. NPDs make changes only when their world starts to collapse.

Most NPD is identified as male. However, some of the NPDs are women. They are very attractive, offer structural support to their children (like nice clothes, great house, cars), but don't really care to bond. They are superficial. They tend to compete with their daughters, especially as they age. Women NPDs often, from my perspective, do more damage than men if they are in a heavy emotional caretaking role. If mother is NPD, she does not care to emotionally attune to the child's needs. The child will recognize support that isn't really present. Children pose as awards for these persons, especially if the kids are successful. If a father is NPD, he will likely be a workaholic and absent, which will hurt his relationship with his children as well. However, if mother is not an NPD, the children have someone to whom they can experience real emotional support. The opposite also applies, if mother is NPD, the hope for the children is that the father can emotionally engage in a healthy way.

Antisocial Personality Disorder:

First of all, this isn't what you think it is. It's worse. This is not someone who isolates from social contact. People often say, "he's so antisocial." That's what people automatically say when someone isn't all that social. However, APD, or Antisocial

Personality Disorder, is the opposite of that. They disarm by charm and are very social. They can be witty and intelligent. They possess a nauseous combination of skillsets that can rob you blind. APD is the person that steals your credit card number. They can also rob you with a gun. Basically, they do not respect laws and figure the only person that matters is them. They can fake empathy towards others, but they don't have it. It is entirely difficult to treat, because they value intelligence, and like to outwit providers and other persons of authority. The Antisocial Personality disorder is someone who doesn't have regard for others. They lie, they steal, hurt animals, and have multiple legal involvements. This is a criminal mindset. APD's usually have been raised and mistreated by others or raised with a lack of empathy or emotional regard. Dog eat dog. Take advantage of or be taken advantage of. This is a very serious personality disturbance. Mass shooters are examples of APD. APD has no empathy or regard for others. They don't avoid others. They misuse, take advantage of, or harm others. They can also be very socially engaging. There isn't value placed on anyone else's life except their own. All you have to watch is crime stories, and you get a clearer picture of this personality.

PERFECTION:

Society likes to feed off the idea of perfection. Perfection in my opinion is both a social and academic paradigm. The academic world devised a way of ranking the student from A's to F's, as a measure of a child's likelihood of success. It is but one measure. However, it failed to integrate the concept of motivation, determination, or social strengths. How is it the non-students or poor ranking students end up successful? The academic world is just one venue or measure of success. If you think that's the only one, then you have a bad case of tunnel vision. Society loves the idea of perfection—as if there is an award ceremony at the end of your life. Actually, at the end of one's perfectionism run, you find more people didn't like them because their judgments and rigid style of thinking, and nothing of course, is ever good enough or up to their standards. I guess no-one likes the constant rising of the bar, the competitive nature, and the divisiveness it promotes.

More people have gotten physically ill or mentally unbalanced because perfection is what they wanted or believed that they needed to have. Try to identify a person you admire because of their perfection. Doesn't happen. Business moguls don't use the term. They WOULD if it really mattered. They probably value innovation or marketing trends more. There seems to be an inverse or opposite relationship between perfection and mental calm. Mental calm promotes problem solving, whereas perfection just grinds up nerves and kills resiliency.

Unfortunately, I believe that perfectionism is more of a gender breeding disorder linked with women, with the desirability factor about as great as wanting an STD. Not that men can't have it (perfectionism), it is just more pronounced with women. As a society, we watch reality shows that are mostly vanity driven. How we lose hours and days of our lives to something that isn't real. What one person notices and what another does not. Trying to come up with universal features of beauty is too restrictive. There are different types of attraction that include, but are not limited to the internal as well as the external, such as intelligence, physical attractiveness, or the spirit of a person. For instance, laughter is an attractive trait, and describes the spirit of the person.

Women tend to believe that perfection is attainable, especially younger women. "If my house is big enough, if my children go to the best schools, and if I am part of this fundraiser…" These are just a few examples of social lies we sell ourselves. When you are fed daily lies, you don't recognize how distorted you get. A little Botox, a little more Botox, big Botox, a filler, a tummy tuck, a butt lift, a face lift, etc. You start to lose your baseline. Big houses don't make happiness, nor does being a size two. Social lies become personal lies, and personal lies kill people.

Perfection is a fear-based reactive mechanism. For example, if you see me as perfect, then you can't say anything bad about me. That's a lie too. If people want to give you a hard time, then they will anyway. Money can't save you from it, nor can beauty or intelligence. Judgment can be fierce. The people who know it most are the ones handing it out on a regular basis. "Did you see how big she got?" They are also the ones who are constantly socially ranking others. Newsworthy: there are plenty of men who have left beautiful women. There are men who have broken up with beautiful women. Why? Skinny won't save you from being dumped or cheated on. There are plenty of overweight women who have husbands that love them and don't cheat on them. Weight does not determine your level of relationship success. Physical beauty can only take you so far. Superficial and selfish aren't big selling points in either gender, and phony or superficial isn't big in the attraction department. It can take a while, but over time, people figure your phony out. Is your need for perfect ruining you? Is it defining you? Does it make you phony? Do you act differently around different people?

I never met a perfectionist that knew how to cope with adversity. I mean cope with negative events that are completely out of their control. If a perfectionist is given a syllabus or educational platform to follow, then they are ahead of it. They get the "A;" however, events that they cannot control are problematic. They are problematic because they ultimately believe there's a syllabus, a YouTube video, or an expert to a control a situation. Educational systems taught us to reach for the "A" and said that if you take this curriculum you will get this degree. Advanced education was a security and you became the Goldstar Elite. But how many Goldstar Elites can't think outside of their own box? There are no awards for common sense, but there should be. Life doesn't guarantee that Goldstar success that universities and other large strata systems are trying to market. . Common sense should be equally marketed. How many people have book smarts but lose their grounding when things get messed up? Experience in a sector separates those that think they know what they are doing from those who actually do know what they are doing. It wasn't ever built on perfection. There were plenty of mishaps along the way. The world we know wasn't just erected by educational giants. It was also built on natural intelligence (schooled or unschooled) and natural talent. A good history of experience shouldn't require a formally educated sponsor.

The Beauty of Failing:

There are plenty of self-employed business people that develop from hard work, trial, some failure opportunities, and perseverance. Failure is nothing more than an opportunity to figure out what information is lacking. However, in our society it comes as a social reprimand. We abhor any sense or perception of failure! We have been marinated to avoid failure since we were introduced to school systems that ranked and monitored closely our failure potential. There is good and bad in that. Most people unfortunately just feel over scrutinized and evaluated by it. At the end of the day, the most resilient people do not allow that to determine their outcomes in life. I am not a fan of giving kids a paranoid sense of their self-value due to their academic performance or non-performance. It drives Psychological disorder and dysfunction. Unfortunately, it's a well marketed, heavily manipulated, over-indulged paradigm of how we define success; not to mention many of the degrees don't carry a good return on your money.

Let's face it, no systems like failure. Failure is fuel. Without fuel, you don't run. What type of fuel are you using? Fear-based fuel, self-driven fuel, or social-attention fuel? Your fuel source tells a lot about you. It also says how far you will go.

Truth be told, a lot of success is driven by fear. Fear can make a person move. It is not ideal, but it is reality. How many physically unhealthy individuals start to change their habits, once a bad diagnosis shows up? I call that fear-based performance. It's not all bad, but nobody wants to grapple with the negative factors that trigger it.

Yet, failure or some version of it has at its roots in the compost of great things to come. Our screw ups and missed opportunities run through our veins. Think about it. The great inventors and business idealists used it as a vehicle for success. People who have made it out of prison also get it. A mother who had to cope with years of a young adult's addictions saw that all the failure gave them a perspective to open an addictions center to find treatments that work better. Crap can eventually grow crop! Good crop. So, if you are currently eating a crap sandwich, fear not. God understands the purpose behind the crap phase, even if you or no one else around you does. And, God has the power to influence you and those around you to pivot you to success. Even the super narcissist next door driving his power car can't guarantee those odds. God just waits until he has your full attention. And when he does, watch out. All those people who waited for you to fail, lookout! You are anything but failing. They don't get it. They can't explain it. They underestimated the wrong person! They bet on the wrong horse.

Perfectionists are not people who can take a loss. They can't take a hit in the ring. They cannot afford to be wrong. They are excellent at avoiding the ring altogether. The problem happens when they are forced into dealing with things that may not be of their own doing—things that force them into the ring. They have to appear perfect because THEY spend a lot of time judging others. As the saying goes, when you dish it out, you better be able to take it, and perfectionists are walking calculators of social risk. They can give you better odds than the Kentucky Derby betting junkies on which behaviors pay off. (By the way, they will not be the longshot bet). They will always play the favorite. Conformity and social insurance is the known currency. They may become a pinnacle of achievement, but they will not necessarily be an innovator or ground breaker.

Perfectionists are superior at calling all the shots, "they can control." Perfectionists are great critics towards others. They don't just point them out, they shove them up your nose. Ask anyone who's related to one of these fine individuals. Not only are they ornery with ridiculous expectations, but perfectionism is a banal pursuit. No one loves you for it. Perfectionists make the IRS 400 page return look lazy. When you don't want others to pick on you, you become the role of perfection. If you appear perfect, you can't be judged. Wrong. We like to say we are good enough because we are not like this person who has a drug habit, or the person who lived on the streets. I don't care what pit you are climbing out of, but perfection doesn't work, and failure experiences actually teach. When the Great Depression broke out in 1929, the people who were jumping out of windows, weren't the money poor. The rich people killed themselves. Why? Because they learned that money defined their existence, their tastes, and their habits. Without it, they had no step-up on someone else. Lack of money would cause a person to become dim or ordinary. The rich who killed themselves never really learned how to operate outside of a wealth perspective. So they did not develop resilience. Their money defined their life in entirety. In contrast, people who had lived broke before relied on their wits as they had before, and they could fight the good fight again. They knew the importance of staying in the ring. And, based on history, the economy came back, and we live, because our ancestors were fighters. Maybe they didn't get the opportunities to belong to prestigious organizations. They were busy surviving. But survive they did. Yet, they received no gold star status. Survival superseded perfection. Failure and mistakes give you a better return on your money.

THE IMPERFECT STORYLINE:

Stories that most of us like are the imperfect, long-shot success stories. I don't know about you, but when I read an Autobiography, I'm interested in personal struggles, not their perfect life. An example of a long shot success is Arnel Pineda, the singer for the rock band Journey.

Arnel has an amazing voice that closely mirrors that of the icon Steve Perry. The group Journey struggled for years finding a replacement that could carry the vocals of Perry. Arnel has been the lead vocal for the past ten years, but it is his path to the band that was amazing. He was raised in the Philippines. His mother had a strong influence in encouraging him to sing. By the time he was 14, his mother died and the family went bankrupt. He lived on the streets in poverty. His friends recognized his singing talent and had him singing for meals. He participated with several bands and did covers for other bands. Journey found him from a YouTube video. He brought the old vocals of Steve Perry back and brought a resurgence of success for Journey. With his YouTube interviews, he reports having a history of shyness, a period where alcohol and drugs were taking over, but ultimately battling his demons to ricochet to success on an international stage against all sorts of odds. If you witness his singing and performance, it is amazing. A long shot story from poverty to becoming frontliner in a historic band that he helped propel once again into superstardom.

Your roots and circumstances are not an indicator of how successful you are going to be. Your ability to fight your inner demons, your motivation, and your perseverance are greater factors. A higher power or the universe is just waiting for you to get on board. Once aboard, the impossible, the improbable, and the unlikely, all become the likely and the empowered, which is what rewrites history.

Relationship Hooks and Getting Stuck with Herpes:

First of all, this is not actually about the status of Herpes. It's more or less an analogy of how things that seem so good, can end up so bad.

There are many books out on "how to catch a man." There is a prolific amount of books because there is a huge amount of interest. Here's the main thought, if you have to work that hard to keep a relationship going (keep it interesting, look runway beautiful, or carry a platform of indifference,) what would you do when you actually marry it? If that person is only interested in you when you are playing hard to get, then what does it mean when you are home stuck changing diapers? When you become less interesting, it's possible that they also become less interested?

If he's only there for the good times, pay attention. He may have charm, the right body, the right brains, and the right connections, but if he dumps you when you are sick and puking in the toilet for something else to do, what do you really have? Very similar to a girlfriend who wants to spend time with you until she gets a better offer by someone else. When that comes along, she dumps you for something to do what suits her better. Why spend more time with her?

This applies to women and men alike. There are self-serving women, we call them "gold diggers," and self-serving men, whom we call "players."

He or she may want some "spark" in their life, outside the responsibility of homelife. That can be found down the block or the next cubicle over.

Marriage has nothing to do with dating. So, as a society, why we date people makes no sense to me. What, so you can see someone on their best behavior? What are they like with high pressure demands, like paying bills, doing laundry, putting yourself last to take kids to the baseball field? That's more important information than dating can give you.

Some people live for newness and the next "high." Playing mind games to get a relationship generally does not bode well for retaining in it. That's a lot of work. The return on the investment might not be all that great. All that means is that you might be sorry that you stayed in the relationship in the first place. Not everyone who likes the chase is worth hanging onto. The people who like the chase, tend to get bored easily—no matter how hot you look. Boredom usually translates to wanting other people's attention too—people beside you. Not instead of you. Beside you. Get the1x2picture?

Then there are people who may not look the most attractive or dress to buy out Barney's, but they have a big personality and can empathize with others. They can compromise. It's not all about their agenda. They are authentically interested and offer help. They probably don't shop at Brooks Brothers. They are not overly preoccupied with your style or brands either. They don't chase names or tags. They don't chase anything; period. They know what a pair of jeans and old boots wear like. You can have a genuine friendship. Boredom is not a concern because the relationship isn't built on what you have or what you don't have. It has a natural flow to it. It doesn't ride on drama or sensationalism. These relationships tend to build a sense of reliability to them. People place high value on them and generally go to great lengths to keep them.

Relationships that go down like a bank heist or smash and grab don't necessarily make the long haul. The sex may be fabulous, but it doesn't guarantee any length of happiness. Physical attraction statistically doesn't hold up long in a relationship, but the personality differences do. If someone violates your way of thinking, they eventually get unattractive pretty quickly. A real relationship requires them to see you at your best and your worst. Not just with your heels and makeup on. See how they respond to your anger outburst, your four letter monologue, your crazy parents, or your hyperventilation that led to a panic attack at a restaurant. Now there's some information. Were they there? Did they care? Smash and grabs are there for the good times, they don't like to be weighed down by anything. That includes your imperfect life.

Pirating, the act of looking for lost treasure, is still a collective interest today. By pirating, I mean chasing down wealth, titles, and success. People call them "Gold diggers". Pirates are on the sniff for coin. For many, it's a way of life. I also refer to these people as "f" ingupward" As in, they only sleep with people who move them up the ladder. Pirates will give you what you want, as long as you give them a lifestyle, status, and things. Once the things are gone, or you are no longer the social diamond they thought you were, they are sizing up someone else's things—physical and otherwise. Prostitution, in my opinion, is at least more honest in its intent. Pirates are not known for their genuineness or loyalty nor do they struggle to go out of their way for you. When it's not convenient, or doesn't come back to them in some way shape or form, they won't be there. They will try to come up with failed excuses that sound good, but teaming up with a pirate (male or female) will always leave you on the short end of the stick emotionally, and definitely short on cash. Trades are trades. If you choose to be a pirate, there is a good chance that the other person is equally on the take. As they say, there is no honor among thieves. They should also add no real loyalty either.

The myth that conflict destroys a relationship:

So, many people offer in as a way of describing their relationship "we never fight." This is somehow viewed as a complete positive. Usually it isn't. Some people don't know how to manage a difficulty, so they just go underground. Things get buried to the point of no return. Where it's easier to walk away than it is to work through. Passive sighing or avoidance can be palpable. The cabinets are falling off their hinges, but no words follow. Silent treatment can be loud. The common answer "no, nothing is wrong." The reality is that what kills relationships is the inability to work through conflict. It's easy to process issues in the high point of your relationship. But what about when you are under chronic stress? Believe it or not, there are people whose marriages have faced bad events, and they have still found a way to stay together. Ultimately, the people whom we feel the most comfortable with are the relationships where we can disagree and still pick up the phone. You recognize differences, but can still retain a functional aspect of a relationship. According to John Gottman who has spent decades of his career focused on marriage therapy, most couples don't break up from affairs. They break up from negative or disintegrated communication patterns, and lack of emotional support. Surprise!

How to destroy a relationship:

The use of emotional excess, lack of emotional presence or indifference, spending abuse, substance abuse, joblessness, poor verbal or absent exchanges, intrusive family, communication walls, negligent or destructive parenting habits, or financial control issues. This list obviously excludes extreme behaviors such as physical or sexual abuse. I would say emotional abuse too, however, I have seen that term get completely manipulated, depending on the honesty of the person speaking of it. For instance, if you are a spenda-holic, and your spouse calls you on it, that DOES NOT mean you are emotionally abused. You may be entitled, defensive, and unable to take any feedback. I've seen women manipulate as well as men, so no favoritism there. From my clinical vantage point, these are the LESS obvious pitfalls of relationship, but are very real. Especially difficult, but not always present, is when affairs are exposed. One person may call the other partner a dirty dog for their affair, but what most people don't know is the side brew of nasty behaviors that the cheated on person may need to own up to. In other words, there may be a distinct behavior that causes the appearance of the breakdown of the relationship, but these "side" habits slowly turn into unrecognizable, big problems. People are pretty good at not owning them either. These are great as kindling to get affairs started. Behind big problems, in my opinion, are "side" problems that are destructive. It's like owning a beautiful house and having carpenter ants hollowing out the inside. So, no matter how beautiful the house, it no longer stands or serves.

What is emotional excess? Emotional excess is a high degree of emotional sensitivity or state of chronic emotional distress. When a person does not understand this, the partner DOES owe it to the other partner to acknowledge this and help pursue therapy or medical supports. If your emotional states are causing fights and/or disruption, it is not fair to assume that your partner can manage this piece for you. It is your responsibility to get therapeutic and medical support to assist in improving your own quality of life. Partners are good as support, but they can't be a ventilator for you. Your significant other should never be your ventilator. As humans, we have different needs that should be met with different supports—not just one. From family and friends to spiritual, intellectual, and physical guides. I often point out that the pressure to make one person reconfigure and support you 100 percent unrealistic. Do you not have different friends for different reasons? Are there some people that you share certain types of experiences with and others you connect with on a totally different level?

Lack of emotional presence is being absent. Not being physically present is one thing, but not being emotionally present is another. Both are tough, however, the latter is far more insulting.

Emotional indifference is the equivalent of talking to air. Your responses don't really matter, which gets painful and leads to avoidance. When this occurs, most people start to go about the family business without checking in. Focus on the children, as to what would appear to be a most legitimate cause, eventually gets "found out" when they leave for college. Empty nest is a very real psychological phenomenon. When your efforts and daily structure has been devoted to helping put others first and your purpose is no longer needed in that specific venue, then you begin to challenge your worth and course of direction.

Spending abuse can go in either direction. You can have a spendthrift who won't allow you to purchase reasonable things. You can also have a partner who spends with little regard for your ability to manage it, hiding and opening up numerous credit cards leading to debt. Joblessness can happen to anyone, but chronic disregard or lack of motivation towards financial support is an issue.

Poor verbal exchanges, with little emotional connection, and lack of intimacy can eventually put you on a dissimilar platform.

The stickler is usually seen when one party decides that he or she is less interested in the other party and has an affair. If a husband is having an affair at work, the wife may threaten to call his boss. The problem with this type of exchange is that it is never forgotten. Threats show you how willing the other party is to smear you. Threats are different from general conflict. Emotional blackmail is meant to discredit or smear. Therefore, a person who tells everyone, including the children, about their partners affair, does it out of vendetta. It doesn't benefit anyone, and if anything, it distresses the children. You are attempting to make the children alienate their relationship with the other parent. Affairs should not be the business of your children. If you want an ally, that is understandable, go seek the support of a trained professional (not three generations of family loudmouths). Children may favor the wounded party initially, however, they may also come to resent the parent that dumped and tried to derail their relationship with the other parent. I have heard spiteful spouses say, "well they have a right to know." I have seen spaces where that has bitten them in the backside, because the motive was ugly. Eventually, ugly motives are unveiled for what they are. Karma and time reveals the true character of both parties. It can take years, but in the spiritual domain, nothing is ever lost or forgotten. What we do today, shows up tomorrow—for good or bad.

Unfortunately, in the case of an affair, rather than dealing with the situation at hand with a trained professional, the wounded party tends to lash out. Calling up the third involved party may feel good for a few minutes. But, your problem isn't the other party. Your problem is the person who is married to you. You can hate them all you want. By doing so, you may think you have broken up that relationship. Sometimes that happens. Sometimes it doesn't. Telling your husband that he spends time with a "loser" woman is only going to make him resent you under his breath. Is that helping your position any?

Understandably after an affair has taken place, strong efforts at managing a person's phone and time takes place. This is not unusual. However, eventually, if you do not allow the relationship to build some trust in it, then resentment is the only seed that you are sowing. The problem is that if there is a chance at having a repair in the relationship, it will be gone. So, you may feel violated or wounded in the relationship and you may feel validated by what you are doing. That is fine. But, please don't expect your partner to pursue a relationship with a vendetta seeker or a controller. Accountability and healthier communication can occur in the form of marriage therapy. The hope, is that if there is going to be any repair, then the smear campaigning and controlling behavior has to stop. Once, again, this is done best with trained professionals, not with a Polygraph machine. If you feel that your spouse needs a polygraph, then perhaps it's better to leave the relationship than spend endless hours "pursuing the truth."

Pursuing the Truth in an Affair:

Unfortunately, I have witnessed time and time again, a victimized partner who wants every detail to the affair. I mean they DEMAND details. The doer of the offense feels the need to oblige. The person feels if they have the facts, then they can find some way to come to terms with it. I've seen nothing but destruction come from the wounded party, playing and replaying horrible images in their head. Often, they would say, "I need to know the whole truth." My recommendation is "you have enough of it already." People struggle with images in their mind, and it can go on for months and years. So, if some therapist states that it's all about being honest, at least be prepared for the flip side. Simply put, there is a certain amount of truth that is not helpful and not healing. Knowing how he kissed her isn't going to help you heal. I think the root of these questions is, "are you more sexually satisfied with someone else?" That may be a more valid question. Repetitive, security type questions are a lost cause. If you need a Fort Knox case, you need to leave. Your brain will never let it go. Cut your losses before all you gain is anger and an enemy. You may be self-righteous; however, if you have children, then making an enemy out of your co-parent is a very bad idea.

Although, when a person has an affair, that person is perceived as "the bad" party. However, most clinical therapists don't necessarily buy into the "bad" party ideology. Although, it is agreed that it is a destructive symptom. Affairs are usually a sign of double fault in the relationship. Refer to the earlier list of destructive behaviors that can be the side brew. That side brew can get very ugly. Side brew behaviors don't make you a saint to live with, and those behaviors are still going to be a problem because they are exposed for the negative that they are. Unfortunately, sometimes an affair reveals the toxicity of the relational system, and can start the a healing process.

I believe the exception to that is serial affairs or multiples. That speaks more of an addiction or a lifestyle choice. Working through repeated situations can really call into question the healthiness of the relational dyad.

Examples of more subtle destructive patterns in relationships that can be a trigger a relationship breakdownare, but not limited to the following: a self-serving personality, lack of help or reciprocity in the functioning of the relationship, being overly needy, entitled expectations, anger/rages, "nothing is ever good enough," suffocating behavior, unreasonable demands; i.e. her parents are always in my house, having a financial Gestapo, over the top jealousy, manipulators, lying over small stuff, etc. So, there are many paths to destruction of a relationship, but all of these identifiers are rarely named, but are CRITICAL destroyers of intimacy.

Unsurprisingly, most clinicians who work heavily in this venue understand that what most people SAY what they would do is not necessarily what plays out. The people who have a commentary on your marriage, or what they would do, is very DIFFERENT when it happens to them. The reality is that there are many factors to consider. It's not a simplistic equation, especially when factors such as children, assets, health stability, and lifestyle are involved. The numbers support that many couples have redirected or figured out what is not happening, and work to improve their relationship.

Five myths about cheating by Eric Anderson in 2012 mentioned statistics about cheating and affairs in marriage. Ranges on cheating varied widely, mainly because people don't like to report that type of behavior. So, if anything, the leanings would be an underestimate. Seventy-eight percent of men he interviewed who cheated, only a handful (small amount) said they were near the end of their emotional relationship with their spouse. Translation is that the majority of cheaters were still attached to their wives. That means that they were not interested in a divorce.

Gross or Net?

People are usually very vocal about how detrimental cheating behavior is. The behavior itself, is problematic. But we are a society that does not always see a full interactive picture. Someone may be silently pushing you away, but when the other party acts out, that person is perceived as the bad person. In some situations, it isn't hard to see how the affair occurred. However, I have never been a fan of blaming one party. What to do after an affair occurs is not always very simple, especially when livelihoods, children, and responsibilities hang in the balance. For instance, if you are in your twenties and encounter this behavior in an unmarried, un-finance tied situation, then your answer is pretty easy. However, if you are married and have sacrificed your professional position to stay at home and raise your children, then this becomes a much bigger issue.

Often the situation can become a Rubik's cube. Providing an answer on one side, doesn't mean the other side can be effective or function. Also, what people assume they see on the outside isn't necessarily the side that the married partner receives. What you see is not necessarily what the other person receives. Every person has their opinion. However, that opinion may not suit or easily apply to your reality. That type of information gathering lacks a lot of detail. It is the equivalent of judging a person's success by using their gross income instead of their net. The gross looks like the whole story, but the net that tells the real story of where a person is at with their finances.

For instance a statement such as this is common. "Women love my husband…he's the life of the party, but they don't have to deal with the drinking, constant criticism, and attacks that I get at home." Keep in mind, this same statement can be flipped about women. I've spoken to men, who have complained of demanding and ugly behavior such as "She keeps filling out credit cards, and I have to pay them."

What this shows us is that you need a full context of a relationship, before you get too intertwined with the "good" or "bad" person narrative. Women can exhibit destructive patterns in the relationship as well as men. Professionals use a broader and wider range of information than your Aunt Sally or your friends.

Control:

As human beings, we prefer to have some sense of control over our lives. Control can give us a perceived sense of security.

However, there are people who take this to an entirely different level. People may make a joke about being "a control freak," but if you ask the people that surround them about this, it is quite unpleasant to deal with. Simply put, a "control freak" has no problem pressing into your boundaries to ensure their security. They want to ensure that their needs are met, and usually whatever means that are needed for it to occur is fine. That is where it becomes dangerous. Arguing with a spouse and following them from room to room. It is beyond an organizational style. It is a "do it my way or I will be adversarial and escalate with loud, uncontrolled behavior." Crying can be used as a form of manipulation when someone is cornered. Control is a kind word for manipulation. Often, people feel that they have good reasons to try to manipulate an outcome. Some parents try to manipulate who their children date, what college they attend, etc. by offering up side distractions or other reinforcers. People do this in marriages. It's not cute, it's not acceptable, and eventually gets seen for what it is. The biggest challenge is when manipulation becomes very rewarding for the doer. They probably found a way to bury a purchase on a shared charge card. Manipulators don't stop until they are confronted and possibly face the termination of the relationship. When you see a person as manipulative, then you want to see what the ultimate goal is. Is it to take over someone's time, take over someone's finances, and feel powerful? Instead of having a healthy discussion, manipulators or many control freaks would rather engage heavy artillery. If the person complains that they just want to have a sense of security, then that person needs to find different methods of implementing their own measures to ensure internal peace. Placing others on the string of their behavior providing self-calm for the control freak is impairing for all involved. If necessary, counseling and medication needs to be introduced.

Bad things CAN happen to good people:

There is a large amount of the population that actually believe that bad things only happen to bad people. This implies a sense of justice. "You asked for it…you got it." That's fine when it fits. However, a lot of times, bad things can happen to good people. Generations of people were imprisoned for bad accusations and bad agendas before we had DNA. There are many people that got executed because of the same.

Life doesn't always offer fairness or justice.

The life of some folks is a battle just getting born. They had every roadblock imaginable. They may have been born to a drug-addicted mother or been exposed to malnourishment, poverty, or abuse. That doesn't make them any less valuable as a person than the child born into warmth, wealth, and resources. Neither child earned the position. It was the handout they received. The truly significant thing here is what they themselves did or attempted to do to improve their well being. There are wealthy young adults that don't amount to much, because not much was ever expected of them. Whereas, a young adult who faced adversity may learn what is valuable faster, and how to self-motivate, which becomes key as they work themselves up the ladder. People who became successful by the sweat of their own brow always amaze us.

The point is simple. Life is not a fair playing field. One person cannot catch a break from multiple hardships or losses. Another appears to have an easy ride and smooth sailing. Tragically, we cannot equalize all fields. The cards and the hand that we are dealt at birth, along with supportive or unsupportive parents, attitude, motivation, role models, financial well being, and general health are all factors that create or discourage healthy and adaptive functioning. The point is simple. Some people are given a relatively free ride with good cards early on. Others have to fight for everything they have. We should not take credit for something that was earned by your grandparents' sweat/labor and good business judgment. You didn't earn that. It was given to you. That doesn't make you better than a person who had an 8th grade education with intelligence but no opportunity. Similarly, there are many people born into difficult situations that fight their way through (as opposed to defining themselves as less than). They don't complain about their fate. THEY deserve credit for the fight at the improvements that they themselves brought to the equation. I am not talking about just citing a victim mentality. Some people stay in that mentality, and choose more of "the world owes me" attitude while others try to make and bring improvements to the equation, so that their children can live a better life. If you are the first person in your family to stop drinking or using drugs, you brought the end to that behavior pattern. You deserve credit for that. No matter how big or small, every piece you modify matters. AND you can own that, and feel proud of that.

What Defines You?

Your circumstances can define you to a point. However, your mental desire and perseverance can outweigh any obstacles or limitations that you may face. This is easily seen in young vets returning from war with missing body parts. Mental fierceness can keep a person in the game and help the body fight to heal faster. Obstacles are like resistance bands. You learn how to work around a disadvantage for betterment. You may trip and fall, but each time you fall, and you learn something new. As long as you are learning, there is no focus on failure.

Often times our bad times, help build us. Why? Because they make us rethink our steps. You have to question. You don't take things for granted. Bad times often can cause us to build new spaces. Tough spaces build resilience. Emotional muscles are built under pressure. So you might as well stop wishing for the light handout. Resilience is NOT built on the "perfect" life. And, generally you don't deserve credit for accomplishments when you don't have skin in the game. For example, if you married someone wealthy, then what did you do with the money? Did you invest it? Did you invest it in others? If you had minimal money and were from a single-parent household, did you put effort into the emotional, physical, and spiritual raising of your child? There are many ways to improve outcomes, even in small ways. Emotional support is a huge gift. Having a sense of a tribe is equally positive. We need to feel that someone cares about our bad times and is there for you when you made a super bad decision. Do you even know who you would call during the bad times? Is the love that you receive

CONDITIONAL? Real life often gets confused with REEL life. The REEL is referring to film and Hollywood style movies and presentations. People unfortunately build expectations about love from Hollywood movies. That's not real. None of the characters lie, get someone else pregnant while they are with you, wreck your credit, fake they have a job when they don't, or refuse to work. In real life, these complaints are not imaginary. Just give me one romance movie about a partner that does these things and they still fall in love. Romance movies are extremely idealistic. Nicholas Sparks, the author, is expert at cuing into the female relationship NEED department. He's been a high profile romance writer that accesses the wishful, but not necessarily real relationship. Real relationships have to work through things. Perfect emotional attunement is not real, but good emotional attunement is. Hope for the best, but really plan on the work (especially in longer term unions) to keep the connection in a better space.

Judgers and Spectators:

The world unfortunately is full of a lot of people who have a lot to say, but lack the expertise to open their mouth. Expertise is negligible. It used to be that in order to comment on something, you had to have a level of knowledge in that subject. But not anymore; anyone with vocal cords and tweet can speak. That doesn't make it helpful or bring to the greater good. We live in an open mic system. Some of it is helpful communication. Much of it isn't.

Being a spectator can be fun. You just sit and observe. However, when you sit back and neglect to help someone that you can, it becomes dark. At those times, spectating is at best neglectful and at worst evil. We just spectate or become career gossips or career critics.

How simple for us. How hard for the person who is trying and doesn't feel successful. Social media can be anything but social. It can be mean-spirited, fake, and targeted. I'm a fan of Karma. I try to guard my own by trying to improve myself. Only God knows the path of a person. It takes age, wisdom, and stupidity to figure out that maybe we should just try to take a higher path.

Go Vertical:

Nobody on this life journey is perfect. There is nobody who hasn't screwed up. Maybe you wrote the book on screwing up. So what? God knew what your screw ups were going to be long before you made them. If you aren't comfortable with the word "God," then substitute it with higher energy, universe, etc. God or higher energy works in all spaces. He doesn't elect to hang out at the country club. God doesn't care how low you've gotten. When you don't feel like you have anything to offer. Or maybe you are thinking about ending it all? God operates in those spaces too. The requirement isn't a particular religious prayer, it is honestly seeking help. If you believe that you have burned every bridge. Don't worry. The biggest bridge maker is God. Not your boss, your spouse, or your neighbors. God can move favor in your direction in a moment's notice. You do have to ask for the help though. You need to ask with an honest heart. Some of the best story outcomes come from on your knees and sometimes from a jail cell. Maybe this is where you have to be to start. So, remember you always have value in God's eyes. You always did and you always will. He is a God of mercy and a God of compassion. You don't need to read the Bible or the Torah, or whatever religious doctrine you subscribe to. God is available to all.

I've spoken to people in the heat of dark moments, just to ask God for help and guidance. Messengers come in all sorts of formats. Although, I've never heard God specifically talk to me, I have seen him communicate with me through others. When you stop trying to control all the stuff you can't control, you might as well decide to hand it over.

We are all led to believe that we can be in control. Take a look around. Do you see horrible events happening? Things that we cannot justify, ignore, or pretend. There is much darkness in the world. But, yes, you do have a connection with the divine. Whether you can see it or not is irrelevant. If you read-up on near death experiences, people describe this whole other entity operating that we term the soul. The soul is active, whether or not our physical body is. You have a cord to the divine; even if you never felt it. So how can you access it?

For starters, if you are in a very dark space, and are pretty hopeless, ask God to send a messenger whom you can hear. Brace yourself. Messengers don't necessarily come in the package you expect. No Fed Ex here. Nope. God doesn't care about form. If he wants to reach you, he will use anything or anyone in your path. God can be a Master of disguise. As they say, there are angels that walk among us. Just ask someone who was in a near fatal accident who was supported physically and emotionally before EMS came. People describe these people, and yet no-one ever saw them. ("*Guideposts*" magazine speaks of these types of encounters with the divine).

The Dress Messenger:

When my father died suddenly, I was pretty young. On this day, I had to accomplish a required task—finding a dress for my father's funeral. By design, I went alone. It became all about the dress, not so much about me, but about the fact that I needed to park my traditional casual style and come up with something that would represent him. I didn't want to mess that up. My father was private, but he may as well been famous for mostly his acts of kindness to random people. He grew up poor, so ultimately he understood how money, or lack of it, can mess people up. His death was a knockout 1-2 punch in my world. Because of his workaholic tendencies, we didn't see much of each other, but he did care about his kids, so that mattered.

I dropped weight like a prizefighter. Intuitively I knew that once he was dead, my support system would crash. It's like knowing you've got a reserved ticket on the Titanic, and you already know the outcome. That's when you know life sucks.

I dragged my body into this dress shop, feeling completely disgusted. Right in front of me, popped what seemed like a Genie in a bottle. There is service, and then there is "THANK YOU GOD, I can't do this" service.

She wasn't pushy. In fact, she looked concerned—peculiar for a sales person. She wasn't pitching dresses at me. She seemed to have more regard than that. She knew by looking at me that the story was something. In the briefest exchange, I told her, "my father died, and I don't know how to do this." The reality was that I wasn't just talking about dresses. All I could really do was wipe my eyes, and smear my eyeliner down my face with my sleeve. I'd just talk and wipe with an oversize, re-worn sweatshirt over and over again. My presence, or my absence of presence, seemed to make this woman tear up. I was pretty young to be that vacant. However, she mirrored my space, and for a little while I wasn't alone. I somehow knew that she knew what my space was without even asking. She stared at me and then looked down. It's like someone gave her a briefing before meeting me. She understood my need. It was in one part about a dress, and the other was just irreparable loss. Her response was so out of the ordinary, that I felt like God put an Angel in front of me to help me out. She seemed to say things that most wouldn't. She opted to say words that made sense to me. The chosen few words mattered. I'm not really convinced that she was a salesperson. I believe, an Angel, was given a summons to try her hand at selling dresses. I will always be grateful to the Angel messenger in the dress shop.

Other Messengers:

I was speaking with a woman who was afraid of not getting the right therapist to talk about the loss of her close friend. She was asking her deceased friend to guide her with some kind of message, but she was still grappling a bit with the internal question. I was getting stonewalled with stiff answers, and all of a sudden, her eyes got big, when she was staring at the dragon fly clips on the shades of the office windows. She said, "those are dragon flies, right?" "Yes they are," I responded. "Those were her favorite, she collected them." This simple dragon fly appeared to be a messenger of support from her friend, that she did find the right person to talk to.

This experience is frequent. Numerous times I came across people unknowingly where they needed a confirmation of sort and received it with hanging words on walls, an unusually styled sentence, or an image that reminded them of someone important. Or even more odd, being able to intuitively dial in to an important subject that was buried. Little oddities help us confirm or disconfirm that we are on the right track. Nature provides some of those opportunities. "He/she loved birds or butterflies. I noticed them staring at me through the window when he/she passed." Another sign that people talk about is finding random loose pennies in their path. "Pennies from heaven" is supposedly a sign from departed loved ones, to show that we are still in their thoughts. There are plenty of stories on the internet about these types of signs/confirmations.

What are confirmations or closures? A confirmation is when you are looking in a direction, maybe for a job, and this person leads you to another, and yet someone very important that ends up assisting you in a big way. A closure, on the other hand, is when you try to reach out, and all you find are doors that either will not open, no matter how persistent you are.

Maybe you find a lot of things, but what you haven't found is a higher space to call upon. Often times, this story has been told and retold, especially in Recovery groups. Disclaimer: if you are not comfortable with the word God, please substitute higher being or Universe. "Once I got on my knees and begged God, if there was a God, to help me. It was then that I felt like I wasn't alone anymore. I started to notice changes in my life." This story is quoted, and should be double and triple quoted for the amount of people who found themselves in such a space. It was there at the threshold of giving up on their ideas, their dysfunction, their co-dependencies, or their kryptonite, that they allowed God into their life to assist them.

The higher element or being or Universe has a topographical map of your life, what's laid out in front of you, and what is not happening or holding you back. What you are sure you need isn't necessarily probably what you need. We have limited vision. We can't see much of anything. We can't see our journey. We can't see the fixed stops along the way—the positive, the negative, and the built in lessons. We do want though. A lot of times, we want the stuff that has left us, abandoned us, or is the only piece that we know of for healing. We want to plug the holes with almost anything to numb out the pain.

God does give us free will to trust him or do it ourselves. Most of the time, we prefer to do it on our own. However, after doing it alone for awhile, you might opt for a higher position, with a better vantage view and greater lateral supports than your ground level existence is offering.

When you are ready, eventually the emotion (art) finds its way to canvas (higher being). It is then that the true shape of its journey becomes known. Among the spilt paint, awkward shapes, and complicated coloring du jour, the soul spills onto the canvas. It is then that the true steadfast form emerges. We didn't need the perfect prototype. We needed the mess. The mess has a divine purpose. The most useless mess has its purpose and calling. We always break down before we build because we need the form to hold and set solid. We don't want to build with errant ideas and faulty internal scaffolding that could drop in a moment's notice. That vertical contact is a method of keeping you supported.

Purpose:

We are all given blessings and burdens in a lifetime. Blessings are just that. A blessing might be meeting your partner at a young age, who remains very positive in your life. It can be your wealth status. It can be your job. Burdens are co-existing problems that continue mostly unresolved throughout your life. Conversely, it can be chronic health problems, chronic addiction, chronic job problems, chronic kid problems, chronic marriage problems, etc. The main issue is that it feels like one step to the positive and two steps to the negative. It generally does not stay stable for any definitive period of time. It also seems that no matter how you try to intervene, you don't feel very successful. No life comes equipped with only burdens and no blessings. What is most important is finding the blessings while navigating the burdens.

Dysfunctional Purpose:

When we fail to find a genuine purpose, we tend to participate in finding a dysfunctional purpose. For example when you can't find a guy you like and end up dating someone you shouldn't. Like a married man or a man that you know will not be emotionally available. That qualifies for dysfunctional purpose. Dysfunctional purpose can come from a codependency. A caretaking need we have. We overextend ourselves. We find new pet projects to fill our time. We obsess with fear. We take pills to sleep. We try to be everything to our partner, kids, or friends. Dysfunctional purpose exists when we note that we are doing quintessentially more for others and scraps for ourselves. Our dysfunction is quietly veiled, so it is unseen, but it is felt. Our personal needs are sacrificed to the core. Sometimes something is better than nothing, at least that's how we justify it. We can go on and on for periods at a time, until our dysfunction gets a universal correction.

Unexpected Purpose:

Well after listening to many stories of people who tried to kill themselves (some more than once), and how there was an "unexpected" intervention taking place. Unexpected might be that someone who was not supposed to come home, showed up. Someone else got a spiritual nudge, and found them in that space. So many people, have taken horrendous overdoses that you shouldn't be able to survive, and yet they do? Why? Because you are needed. Your knowledge, your know-how, your spirit has work here to do. We are here to teach and be taught. Nobody is really responsibility free. The best teachers are often the one's that really know what it's like to mess up. If you have survived what you shouldn't have, it means something. Sometimes, you wake up with no-one to intervene, when you planned on being dead, take note: you matter in the universe.

I've spoken to some people with the understanding that for some reason you survive the un-survivable. Is it luck? I sincerely doubt it. There is a reason that you are still alive. There's a reason, a season, a message, and an outline that you will present to the Universe that matters a lot. You just haven't figured out what the hell it is. So, stop trying to think your job is to end it. The right person, the right situation will present.

Why Bother Syndrome:

Have your dreams been dashed? Your hopes down the sewer? Nothing is what you expected or ordered? Hold on. Lessons are showing up right and left. Not necessarily to criticize or condemn you, but to show you who you are or where you need to be. Hardships may set us back, at least from where we want to be, but there are also blooms that come with those thorns. For example, If your spouse didn't leave you, maybe you would always stay too dependent upon others. Tough stuff makes you internally stronger. Getting taken care of with little worries, can be a plus, but if that person dies, you become vulnerable. When you stop comparing yourself to others, is the first release. Everyone has a different journey, with different timing.

Timing is not all the same for everyone. The problem is we expect to be like everyone else. Get married when everyone else does, have kids when everyone else does, etc. In the universal truth, God or your higher power doesn't care about society's plan for timing. God or universal power knows your timing and your reasons. The problem is that no-one sent you the memo. What if it was planned that way from the get-go? Unlike in the academic world, timing is staged and clear. If you do this, you will get that. Academia may give you a firmer sense of building towards your goal or dream job, but it DOES NOT guarantee success with it. Your success, I believe is based on a universal or higher power determiner. We may want the dream job when we are younger, but we may not have the skillset, experience, or contacts to really develop it. So, we bite our teeth on smaller spaces and build from there.

We teach everyone that there's only certain ways to learn, certain measures of success, and all timing should be the same. But the higher universal power does not care about any of that. That's why the guy with experience in the landscape profession got the commercial bid and you did not. He built his experience from the ground up. Maybe he never went to college, but all the information he needed about building a business was near (access). So he got to learn through others experience and what they taught him about business. He probably worked for other people long before he started working on his own. He probably didn't learn about how to do a bid from a book. He probably learned it the hard way. The guy with the educational theory, may understand the theories, but does not have the experience to know the inner workings. So, he may make some mistakes in the bid process that cost him the job.

Why is it that people "catch a break" or meet up with the right person at the right time? Coincidence or not?

Many people believe in coincidence. There are some random coincidences. But I also believe that some coincidences are not so random. Squire Rushnell has written a series of books on what he terms "God winks" These are compilations of stories about life and love that appeared as coincidences that mattered. God winks are loosely defined where at the precise timing, can go one way or another because you meet a paramount person or situation. This is when the doors come flying open with no obstacles. In contrast, when you face one obstacle after another, and you keep taking on more battles, that may be a sign from the universe or higher power, that this is not where to go.

A common example of this may be a couple. When problems arise in the relationship, you find yourself reaching and reaching to calm a situation, find a new way to resolve conflicts, be more attentive, whatever, but the key word is "whatever" you do, you cannot get any improvement in the situation. As my grandmother would say, "not meant to be." It's just that no matter how much you want the situation to work, no matter how much therapy you get, you cannot keep trying to put a foundation in, if it keeps getting demolished. If that's the case, pay attention, and realize that it's not working for bigger reasons. Maybe you can't make it work because you are supposed to be with someone else. In hindsight, we can see more clearly, but it's so hard to see when you are in the process.

Other situations might occur when you are stuck and need movement, and accidentally end up sitting next to a huge informational source on a plane, who sets you up with an important person. The singer who needs a break, gets found when a high powered management exec, walks in at the precise right place and right time, where he is singing. Celebrities have frequent stories of this variety. Most will tell this story on coincidence and base it on luck. You call it luck, I call it God's help and universal purpose.

This story or some variation on it is heard frequently. "I can't believe I was so lucky!" I agree to disagree. You weren't that lucky. It was the universe or higher power smiling down on you, giving you that lift that you desperately needed to get you started in the right direction.

Often actors/actresses are directly related to celebs by birthright such as parents, cousins, aunts, and uncles. That appears to be the link that was influential. A very influential coincidence, if your hopes are in movies, acting, or theatre. A difference in access and understanding of the business that other people don't have. Yet in those situations, it was set in birthright. When the timing was right, the opportunity and means would be available.

What this implies is that you need to do what you can to help your situation and place the rest of your confidence in a higher space. Prayer or meditation can assist with this. The academic world can provide you with a certificate or degree, but a higher space gives you the opportunity to use it.

The world of coincidence and favor shows us that not all timing is the same. It tells us why some people become extremely successful coming from poor or meager upbringing. The higher power or universal will can turn a cycle of rejection into a pool of favor at a moment's notice.

THOUGHTS TRAPPED BY LIES:

However, sometimes people get their thinking trapped by unintended lies. Lies often are perceptions and opinions, which are everywhere, and are regularly forced on people. Old lies were that professional women could only work as teachers, nurses, and secretaries. People pass down often how they were treated. Emotional negligence, by not being present, creates valleys of separation in relationships. This is the unintended lie. Lots of unintended lies cripple goal-seekers. "You can't do that." "Why?" "Because it has never been done like that before."

In 1973, Secretariat, the underdog racehorse, won the triple crown; which hadn't been done in 25 years. Even more incredible, was that the owner was a woman and a housewife. In 1973, to get Secretariat trained, she had to raise six million dollars. This feat was incredulous at the time, with the additional feat of competing as an owner in a sporting industry that was dominated by men.

Same doesn't define success. Different does. If you are different, great! Talk to the people who have your traits. For instance, a father who is very masculine may not be able to support his son's journey into dance. He may be your father, but his traits are very different, and hearing his diatribe on what he considers a success may be very different from your gifts and talents.

Kevyn Aucoin was a famous makeup artist, early LGBTQ activist, and author. His clients were high-end celebrity models. He was adopted from birth and knew that he was gay by the time he was six years. He dreamed about playing and applying makeup. Back in the day, I'm not thinking his family really understood who their son was destined to be. What kind of son likes playing in makeup? He battled internal demons and damage from feeling rejected at birth. He was raised in the South where being openly gay was not uncommon. His beliefs were not shared or even understood. He was noticed for his differentness. He suffered emotionally for his differentness, and yet God or the Universal power pushed him out of his small world to a large stage with great access to power and prestige. He died in 2002 at 40 years of age. His makeup line is still active and well known. Sephora sells his line. People have had great respect for him as a person. The interviews speak highly of him as a gentle, loving person. He was so successful then, and still is, sixteen years beyond his own death. Kevyn likely never saw himself for who he truly was, how admired he was, and what he did to help others.

He appeared to push past his own pain to attend to help others see their own beauty, and he wasn't transfixed by the external. Many women benefitted from his expertise and wisdom.

I think one of God's biggest jokes is to challenge your perceptions by placing people in your path that are hardships—they don't get you and they challenge your beliefs. It doesn't sound like much of a blessing. But their job may be to learn from you. Not the other way around. Kevyn likely was placed to be a teacher to others about recognizing the spirit of a person, and the influence of a person, as opposed to their sexual orientation. Different can be groundbreaking.

This isn't a road race. This is a journey. Your timing and your gifts and your blooms, may look different than your girlfriend.

Life also throws curveballs and surprises. If you live to acquire fame and fortune, then there's plenty of people who have had it, but are not necessarily finding it the perfect anecdote to all that ails them. Plenty of successful people acquire drug problems (a temporary lift away from their reality). With all the fame and money in the world, people still can live miserable. Some have taken their own lives.

Some people chase external validation with large scale homes and lots of things, while others are chasing internal validation such as inner peace from thoughts that bind them into feelings of hopelessness and inadequacy. In Western society, we chase a bit too much. We do not know how to be. We only tend to understand outcomes. Not process. If you are a human being, you ARE a process.

There are good coping skills and bad coping skills. Bad is defined as in the sense, they create more problems than where you started. What are people chasing for hundreds of years? Inner calm and a sense of internal peace. A lot of battles that look like they require outside answers, are really representative of internal battles. If someone is screaming or raging at you, imagine where they are at in their own self-identity. Finding a new boyfriend/girlfriend or spouse just gives you the opportunity to play out the drama show with a new sponsor. The show really hasn't changed all that much. You just change out the players. Not uncommon and usually just a temporary fix. The old skeletons continue to lurk. You just have an unknown prospector who hasn't come across them yet.

Thoughts create peace or battles. The endless negative mind chatter that loops can become your captor. Don't worry about what someone on the outside is doing to you. Sometimes the biggest enemy is the internal lie or lies that keeps floating around your head. It creates unnecessary battles everywhere, and one lie loops into another. It is a parasitic den of unintended lies woven with truth. None of it is all that tolerable.

How many lies are encircling you and creating a cycle of defeat?

Contracts:

Have you ever met someone and connected by something as simple as a glance? The eyes show depth and can be very responsive. Most people we make and break contact fairly easily. There are others that are not easily explainable— a deeper level of knowing; like they understand without saying much at all. Soul contacts keep us connected. You can hang with a lot of people, but it's different when it's on a soul level. Soul contacts are recognizable because they are very easy to establish and very easy to continue where you leave, even if it is years. It's like that friend that you haven't spoken to in years, but when you do pick up the phone, there's an immediate connection. You don't have to explain the where or the why. The details are not the requirement of the relationship. The relationship or friendship tends to support itself because of a stronger inner principle. Good times are easy, that's like moths to the light. The test is the bad times. Trouble shows up. You fail or you falter? Who can really rise up, shut up, and be present. These are soul contacts.

What I like to tie in are those very few people that you meet unexpectedly, which can be same sex friendships where you feel a connection, but you cannot really explain why. You can't really explain the connection of the friendship, as there are people in your life that it has taken years to build a solid connection with, and then there are those that are contract type of connections. It takes very little. Like they were supposed to be part of the journey all the time. Most people do not know many of these people, but they can describe one or two.

Contract type of connections are internally recognized. Like you feel it when you see it. There's something internal that says "pay attention, this person is important."

There are certain people that will be part of our journey. We love certain contracts, those that are unconditional and loving. Then there are those that are more difficult. It could be described as a longer term difficult marriage. The idea is that there was a certain "predetermination" to this contract. However, most people feel that there are some "contracts" operating in their life.

Contracts are soul-derived connections, but not all of them end positively. Some people say that they noticed the person immediately from across the room. The relationship may have been a contract, but it may have been hampered by a reason or a season. For example, there are some people whom you have a terribly strong attraction to, but they are not good for the long haul. They burn bright and fast, at the start, but fade fast. Friendship soul connections, however, tend to not have as much difficulty. The requirements are different out of the gate.

The threat of not changing:

Maybe you feel like you've been living on the edge for years. A lifestyle that takes much more than it offers. Maybe you run from idea to idea, circuit to circuit—different cities, different faces, and you have road rash. You wake up with the stamp of that rash on your coffee searched, fumbling morning steps.

Unfortunately, the world is full of antagonistic voyeurs, who want to be present to see this space you are in. They also have an opinion about who you have become, and why you should be vegan. If you are a Vegas headliner, then you take on volume shows. Your life in some ways is larger than itself. In other ways, it can be very fish-bowlish. The people in your life you are supposed to be close to just get drowned out in the "make it happen" arena. You may be a CEO of a company, and you don't have the luxury or privilege of letting anything fail. Theory sounds good, but it's reality that makes you make it happen. You make it all happen for good or for bad.

Maybe logically, the only thing you are married to is your career. You may have a family, but you are rarely there. You catch calls where you can. As much as you try to keep grounded, what the job requires, what the family requires, what your finances require, what the relationship needs, it all pretty much falls on you. And when you talk to others about it, they don't really get it. You can tell by the stupid but sincere answers you get. If only, it was that easy, you would have figured it all out by now. The demand isn't the nine to five. It doesn't keep good hours. It never did. Sometimes you think if you could just catch some air, you can ride it out. Eventually, you learn to ride numb, and sometimes you sit amazed that you have been able to hold up as much as you have. The show must go on.

It's the repeated costs in life or the repeated losses that gets us messed up. After a few decades, the soul damage gets rough. You develop habits of avoiding people to avoid the connection. Connection is great, but costs just the same. If you have a strong emotional or physical connection, the cut off feels like crap. Coping habits—good and bad—get co-mingled. Smoking, drinking, shopping, gambling, over-sleeping, or sex. You name it, it's all been done before. Some people self-harm, it has been said to cut off the emotional pain. Physical pain tends to redirect or cut-off emotional pain. Larger surface tattooing is a form of emotional processing or manipulating our pain. Art maybe, but really our storyline. I don't know who developed the concept of the traveling gravestone plastered to the back window of the car. Names, birth date, death date. So, we carry our pain with us. Tattoos too are often our traveling emotional morgues.

How many people are tied to things that keep them barely functional? You are still re-living events from your early past—the love of your life, the biggest loss, or the ongoing loss of your closest relationships. When your RAM space is limited for new experiences; it's official, you are an addict. An addict to the past. That my friend carries mass x acceleration = Force.

If you can't find a good purpose in your life at the moment, you will find a dysfunctional purpose. Keep in mind, it still has purpose, but the purpose is a bit distorted and disoriented. Dysfunctional purpose is our codependency. I don't call you out on your stuff, if you don't call me out on mine. It is a secret agreement leading to dysfunctional purpose. They remain secret, because if you opened your mouth, you would have to face what you are seeing. There is a reason for your defensiveness. Defensive measures are created to keep you functioning or not facing your fears. Sometimes, we help others with their dysfunction, because we, too, have our own operating as well. For instance, why would two addicts come together? Easy. There is no judgment, and they have enough knowledge of the internal space the other faces. A sober person may want to understand that, but internally, understands VERY LITTLE of that. A sober person may make demands upon the addict, that another addict would not dare push. This is just one example of a codependency.

Self-Attack:

We have fierce standards for ourselves that are worse than the ones we have for others. You are the worst on yourself. No room for error or self-apology. You don't let yourself off the hook. You have flashbacks of your words. You only keep them in your head to remind you of what a flake you can be. You can be fast and furious with your mouth. Before you know it, you are in a space of regret. Regret for what you did say or didn't say. Leave or be left. You know the options. The emotional baggage is getting heavy.

Each time you swear that somehow, someway, the "it" that is driving you will be different. You'll stick it out. The problem is your DNA. You see and feel the tsunami by the subtleties, long before it hits. It's your strength. It's your weakness. How can you call out someone, who doesn't stick around long enough to hear it? Maybe leaving is the only thing you know. You don't ever express your sadness or your anger or your discontent. You just carry it.

Self-attack is usually the dirty surface under the scab. You might see the scab, but you don't see the irritant, bacteria under it that won't allow the scab to heal. Most people really don't align with such thoughts about themselves. It's like having a little black mold in the drywall. It's not big, but wow, can it be destructive.

It usually doesn't come rapidly to the surface either. It's not dinner chat. Self-negativity is rarely that tangible to take a hold of. Where you can find it parked, is in the back of your mind. There it has all the comforts and WIFI access to transport it anywhere in a moment's notice. New experiences are contaminated with past Google searches in your head. There it finds images of stuff and everything it grabbed onto. You recognize it by the pit in your stomach.

When was "good enough" really good? Like almost never, right? Or maybe occasionally? You are successful, but you still have a critic in your head that wants to sabotage you. A workaholic tyrant no less. Where do you start? Back in your head where it should get ticketed for double parking.

STOPPING PANIC:

If your brain swirls into panic pretty quickly, then there is something you can do besides grab Xanax or Valium repeatedly. Often panic attacks don't always make sense. They are not all induced based on circumstances. Many simply show up by the brain firing up too much norepinephrine in the system.

"A sudden, rapid rise of norepinephrine can cause panic attacks." "What Norepinephrine Does (or Doesn't Do) for You," Understanding Neurotransmitter Dysregulation, *Verywell Health,* Dellwoo, Adrienne, October 4, 2017. Because of this, panic disorder, really has strong medical underpinnings. Clearly too much norepinephrine will have a host of physical symptoms on top of brain racing. So, what can you do? Some anxiety can be managed, some may not be as easily.

The effort should be made to see if your anxiety could be managed behaviorally. What I found in my early days in practice was that progressive relaxation was not so helpful. If your body is ramping up symptoms quickly, you need to attack it pretty quickly. If you are an expert in breathing, then you can use that to your advantage. However, most people are not exhibiting that level of expertise.

Active, semi-cardio, physical movement does assist in slowing down anxious thinking. I figured this out about 25 years ago with a male client who had repeated panic attacks. At the time, the recommendation was breath work. Needless to say, because of the advanced escalation, the breath work was not effective. Progressive relaxation was a bomb in the midst of an escalating internal panic. I knew I had to redirect the thought process, so since he was good with cleaning, I had him start to vacuum when he was home. I told my colleague about this, and she was completely disgusted with my odd intervention. "Where is vacuum therapy listed?" She says. "Well, nowhere." I just had an internal suspicion that the movement might help create a shift. So, when he came back, I figured my client would carry the deciding vote. Great news, it helped! He was happier because he felt like he might be able to control it better, so his mood lit up. A few less panic attacks was worthy. Then I realized that the adrenaline was so amped up in his body that he needed something to burn it off. The therapy wasn't about vacuuming. The actual activity, with the push and pull on an older, heavier vacuum began reducing the adrenaline that kept recycling into more panic.

In my practice, I modified away from the concept to use a heavier jog in place (instead of walking) with large circle, arm rotations to see if agitation could be slowed down. If you talk aloud during this process, you will be able to get a visual on how your breath starts to slow down, along with your body. This is good news, because a lot of the terrifying feelings in the body that panic and too much adrenaline bring, will start to close down faster. It's like shutting down all the open windows on your computer. As you jog in place, it gradually competes with the panic symptoms, and slows them down.

The action of increasing physical activity during panic, actually sounds like the opposite of what you should be doing.

By increasing activity on one end, it slows down the build-up of adrenaline or norepinephrine that your brain decided to dump on you. The disclaimer to this method is that a person should be in good health. I would not use this type of intervention with anyone who does have any higher risk towards cardiac problems. Always rule out a medical condition first. Once it has been established that this appears to be panic related, then different interventions can be enlisted.

When my clients would panic, I would have them initiate this style of cardio activity to slow it down. You have to slow down the agitation or a person becomes very hysterical. The brain has a very difficult time focusing on negative thoughts and physical activity at the same time. The body focuses only on extremely important tasks first like oxygen to the cells. Less critical tasks get sidelined. The beauty of it, is that most of the time it works, and helps people become less dependent upon Xanax, Valium, Ativan, or Klonopin. However, this activity is not likely to be effective enough when manic level anxiety shows up.

Exercise-a-holics:

Think about some of the friends or relatives you know who keep moving like they have a motor attached. A lot do it for secondary benefit, because it reduces internal anxiety, and stops you from thinking very heavily. It is true that brain neurotransmitters (like endorphins) start being released as well. The brain has to focus on survival needs such as oxygenation and moving blood flow. It really puts thought process into a secondary position at that moment. That's why thought patterns become so much more muted when you are physically active or working out. As an experiment, go try to talk to someone in the middle of a run, and ask them what they are thinking about. Chances are, you won't get much of a dialogue there.

When you are in the middle of a panic attack, however, people usually don't recognize that larger movement and a little cardio will interfere and block it. By larger I mean, a little more rigorous. Such as jumping in place while performing arm rotations for at least a few minutes until you find your breathing slowing down. Your body will not burst apart like it threatens, it will just gradually stop it from over-steeping like a runaway train. (By the way, you can do this in the privacy of your domicile). You don't need to run marathons or walk the neighborhood, especially when you are faced with the adrenaline-dumping, panic attack at 3 am. Don't worry about waking up, you are plenty awake at the moment. Pacing will help a little, but not enough. Lying in a ball on the bed is not effective. When the energy of a panic attack is coming at you, it will require a larger expenditure of energy to shut it down. Interesting, you say? All I know is that it works. Whatever you do, don't just lie there. That's like lying on the train tracks for the train to run over you. That will guarantee misery. Instead, take a hold of it, by engaging in the above. Challenge it physiologically. Work it off aggressively, slow it down, and make it more manageable by facing it and tearing at it. For panic attacks, I think it is much harder to get it calmed through meditation, unless you really know how to implement advanced breathing strategies.

For example, what do you do when the semi competent babysitter gives the four-year-old too much sugar at night? First off, after the child downs a few Oreos, he starts to wake up. He will be extra happy, and maybe spin around a bit. Now if you tell him to sit down and be still; wrong answer. He can't do that. The only chance you have of getting this child back to some calmer space, is to NOT have him try to lie down. You know that won't work. You have him burn it off, until he's exhausted. By doing so, he will think you are super fabulous by not demanding appropriate behavior. But what you are really doing is trying to make him burn up that sugar load at a faster rate. The faster he does that, the better chance you may have of getting him eventually to sleep. The same with panic attacks. You actually have to fight fire with fire. Adrenaline with adrenaline to work it down.

Anger:

Anger isn't bad. It's just information. Oh bullshit you say. Anger is bad. When I release it, it clears the room. Everyone runs for cover. It's got too much energy. It seems to always have an endless source of energy. It also has an endless source of reasons. I have to wait for it to slow down, before I can do anything, you say.

It's what you do or don't do with it that determines how effective you can be. Many people just try to drink it away. At least, when you are drinking, you aren't screaming. Drinking flips the serotonin equation to your favor. It calms you. It slows the anger at least for a few hours. Very few hours.

If talking is toxic, at least then you are not toxic. If you carry anger, it gets a hold of you on the inside. It creates all sorts of opportunities for biological disharmony. Your stomach hurts, your head aches, and your blood pressure surges. Fight or flight. How many times can your body endure that crash and burn?

I'm not saying that you don't have valid reasons. I bet you have some great reasons. Let's just say that you are probably not being unreasonable. Anybody would get ticked off, right? So, let's assume that you are unequivocally correct. What I am saying is the longer that it is carried in you, the greater havoc it gets to run in your life and relationships. It creates medical and social pressure. The head needs a release, so does the body. Anger doesn't offer that release. Your thoughts about it rarely change or give you relief.

First, you have to slow it down. Stop it from building energy. Then you can start separating from the thoughts around it. The truth is that we govern its release. Much of the time we forget that we are the jailer. We have the keys. We feel solid walking around with those keys. We let them dangle. Other people hear them jingling in our pockets. Those keys are loud. They are tightly intertwined. It is a big deal to let go of them. We are paranoid and don't let anyone keep charge of our keys. Because we can't let go of any of it, we are trapped in it, until we realize that we become chained by it.

Sprinters, distance runners, or wavers?

Who are your runners? The supports that help keep you running your journey. They keep you fighting to move forward. They help you fight for position. Sprinters are good for short and fast runs. Maybe get you from point A to point B, but not necessarily to Z. As fast as they are on the scene, is unfortunately, as quickly as they fade out or exit.

Distance runners are generally present for the good, the bad, and the ugly. This may be your spouse, your neighbor, your kids, or your extended family. Maybe your friends or your dog. You only need a few good runners.

Crowd wavers come on the scene when you get popular. Pleasant, but of limited use. They love you when you are on the inner rail or leading. They seem to lose contact with you when things go south. Crowd wavers are not good for trench toughness. In addition to this, they can't or won't help lift when it's heavy. They seem to lose interest rather quickly. Wavers have attention problems because they are comparing you to everyone else, and what and who can provide it better.

Wavers are the type of people who cheer or hand-wave you on when you are successful. They are usually well-groomed, attractive people who like to be in known places. They are very cheerful. This person is charming. They know how to work a room. They know who the sommelier is in the restaurant. They will assist you any way they can, as long as they can see that their relationship with you benefits them in some way—financially, job-wise, or socially. All is good, as long as you can play the role they need you to play.

This works out well, as long as certain criterion are in place. Do not get too old, too physically worn-out, or in need of too much healthcare attention; don't get too fat, don't lose your money, and don't get in a situation where you are in less demand.

Wavers like titles. They want associational gain from you. Technically, relationships are trades of all sorts. However, if you are trading younger looks, then the usual trade is financial or status gain. Once you lose your status, though, it's time for the separation.

Choose to be a distance runner, if you can. Wavers look great, but they are not, as they say in horse world, "built for distance." Out of the gate, they look solid. However, as time goes on, they lose their energy and interest. We need to find as many internally strong, distance runners rather than wavers for term or a season

No Handouts:

Bishop T. D. Jakes, often speaks on when a person is "going through the wilderness." Tough times. He speaks of distant supporters (people who have been on your path, but do not travel the entire path with you), and inner circle people, as well as the divine. Bishop Jakes states that if there is a calling on your life, meaning you are going to excel, it's NOT going to be handed out on your terms. There's going to be very tough spaces that you end up managing alone. People can be alongside, but you have to walk the ultimate paths to success independently. Many people have to walk dark spaces before they can experience their success. If you truly want extraordinary success, you will need to be able to face extraordinary difficulties. Building resilience and the connection to a higher power can create that space.

Resilience:

People often think that resilience is based on success. Meaning that because a person is successful, they make lots of money, they are visible, and they must be resilient. Success doesn't always merge with resilience. Look at the many talented singers that do fabulous on the charts, but cannot deal with their success. They can't seem to get their footing. The resilience is rarely ever built in. The cultural belief is that success means resilience.

However, resilience is based on something altogether different. Resilience is built on wounds. Missed opportunities, errors, and screw-ups. Resilience may not be where you are looking. Success doesn't guarantee that you have it. Many people who are wealthy, aren't necessarily happy.

Resilience isn't about being happy. Resilience is the ability to plunge forward after you've been burned. After your spouse replaces you with someone else, after your child gets killed in a car accident, or you get diagnosed with a terrible disease. There's nothing great about the process.

We look at popular places to see resilience. Sometimes yes. Not always. The homeless person has resilience. How unpopular. We don't consider homeless people resilient, but you better believe many are. People in jail are too. But we don't like to talk about resilience in that space, because it isn't popular. Keep in mind though, resilience isn't built on being popular. It's being able to manage the ugly, and the unexpected, with little to no external guide.

Resilient people aren't necessarily able to predict every potential downfall, but they learn to bend with the wind, instead of cracking. They also stand in spaces that they aren't happy about, but they show up anyway. When your young adult gets arrested for DUI, resilient people manage the crisis. They are already past the "wish this person was more perfect" scenario. They dive in and manage. Diving in doesn't mean they agree. It just means that they are present.

Resilience isn't necessarily about getting the degree. Resilience is managing the business. Learning the positive. Learning the negative. Resilience doesn't have much to do with fairness. It is built from bad spaces and gushing wounds.

In a perfect world, you can make perfect choices. This isn't that place. The point is this that many people say, "I would never do that if I was her." What people fail to see is that some choices are not between polar opposite spaces such as perfect and bad. Many choices unfortunately fall between the narrow segue of bad and worse. There are easy choices to navigate, and others are a complicated choice, because you are short a lot of information at the time, or you are short on resources. Either way, sometimes the choice is "as good as you can get it" because of the lack of good options. For the most part, I never met a woman (in my line of work) who was tolerant of abusive or stupid situations. I've met women who had complicated spaces to navigate with multiple considerations that were none all that easy. So, before you just assume that someone has an easy answer and is just stupid, think again. Most people aren't stupid.

Resilience is about pushing forward WITHOUT focusing on the negative. It's pushing forward despite the negative. It can acknowledge the negative, but it won't take up permanent residence as a victim. There are plenty of people who associate success with resilience. That is not always true. Resilience is the bad actor that shows up to the party. Bad things have happened to them. It's not that they didn't notice. Internally, however, they still want to finish the race. Resilient people can run lean with resources. They may not be able to count on the emotional support or the financial check that will push them through, but they do move forward with whatever they have. It always amazes me, how, for example, a single mother fed a family on using simple ingredients like ramen noodles in a creative way. The success was that no-one starved. She never had the opportunity to buy organic fruits, vegetables, or expensive meat. Keeping your family alive is a basic sense of resilience. There are plenty of resilient people in places that you don't expect.

The difference between someone who is resilient versus someone who is not is that the resilient person learns to develop internal strength. They don't allow others to define them or their situation. Without a doubt, they grieve their situation, but the situation does not define them or bleed them out. They can identify bad situations, but they do not allow themselves to become victims.

Resilience in action:

These days the requirements to get into a good college are beyond stringent. Not only do you have to be a straight four point or better, you must also demonstrate leadership skills, volunteerism, and a strong work ethic, when most adults still haven't figured this out. They say they want the best and the brightest. Well the brightest may lack the internal resourcefulness that the person with the lower GPA may have. Unfortunately there are many brilliant people who don't have much ambition or drive. However, a person who may not score as high, yet still a good viable student, has learned some level of resilience, because it DOES NOT come easy. In Valorie Burton's, "Successful Women Think Differently," she refers to astronauts applying to the NASA program, would have to qualify by "failure" experiences. Why? Because they want someone who is resilient when things go wrong. Not just a person who manages when things are in control and positive. They wanted to HIRE people that failed. They were not idiotic to believe they were hiring failures. They were hiring people, who learn how to trouble shoot on their feet, when it all goes south. They needed someone who can bear the brunt of things not working.

Before you grab all the merits of success, you need to be able to lurk through mess-ups. You may be a very disciplined student, and certainly the discipline and intelligence matters. However, finding resilient students, and students who have failed before and demonstrate their awareness, may be primer to a new grade of success.

Resilience is about showing up and being present in spite of what just blew up around you. Resilient people may ask "why?" but they DO NOT stay there. That does not become the focal point. Resilience is about NOT devouring the bad stuff. Because once you devour it, it can absorb you. The lies and the injustice can reset your sense of value to the negative. Internal poverty is the worst space to carry. Resilient people refuse to accept a negative identification of who they are.

Fear:

When fear is your best friend, you are living with poison. Fear comes to destroy. Fear convinces you that you cannot engage. Fear doesn't operate in isolation. Its intent is plural; go bigger, go broader, and go global. When people are operating from a sense of fear, it usually isn't a singular factor that is causing it. Instead, it presents with a link of one fear to another to another. Fear breeds on more fear. It has total bias. It goes for control. Fear is a control freak. Its function is to try to appear logical, but the connectors are loose. It starts out sounding reasonable, but pretty soon it gets large and convinces you of tales of gloom and doom. "No-one will ever love me," or "Everyone will think I'm a failure." Fear paints terror down every path. It convinces your body to fill with adrenaline and fight or flight. Fear is an offender. It is a violator. It is very suspect, and you have to manage it, or it will try to take you over. Ask anyone who has experienced anxiety reports about fear. It is very real. But, it can also be put in its place. If you want to feel successful in your thoughts and your body, you need to put fear in its place. You have to learn of its moves, so that you can learn to neutralize it.

Fear likes to keep everything locked up. It's the hoarder and orderer of "just in case." Fear focuses on catastrophe. It imagines the unimaginable. Fear restrains, and keeps you in a straight jacket. Fear is the megaphone of "No. You can't do this. You can't do that". No-one would ever believe that you are good enough. Fear tries to remind you that your roots are too simple. "You can't fit in with those people." Fear whispers trash in your ear. It tells you just to stay home. Avoid the people at work. Don't go to the store. People might look at you. People might judge you. Fear is an internal sociopath. If you don't understand how this sick enabler works, it will continue to beat you up. You need to know this attacker. But more importantly, you need to know how to dismantle those fear-based thoughts and reduce the large volume of adrenaline it produces.

CALLINGS:

Everyone has a divine gift or a calling. Some people have no idea what their gift is or haven't fully discovered it yet. However, it is my belief that we all come into this world with gifts. The task is recognizing and using them.

Gifts and talents can fall under the professional domain. They can also fall under the parenting or caretaking domain. You may be a leader or you may be placed in positions that require your ongoing caregiving or support to assist one individual or several. Maybe you are a great cook and nurture your family through preparation of great foods.

Innate gifts such as athletic abilities, dancing, singing, the ability to play musical instruments, creativity, interior design, carpentry, electrical work, painting, the ability to engage in quantum physics, the ability to heal others, the ability to understand medicine, or the ability to provide counsel to others are just the tip of how humans are innately gifted. No matter what the level of success, all individuals have a God-provided genuine talent or calling. Sometimes people are confused as they have a few interests. The surest path to clarification, is to start paddling with whatever catches your interest. If what catches your interest eventually gains more speed or opportunity, you can continue the pursuit. That is called an open door.

OPEN DOORS AND CLOSED DOORS:

Open doors usually have support, reinforcement, and unique coincidences attached to them. "I was just seated next to this woman, and as it turns out, she is a recruiter and head-hunter, and I just decided yesterday that I needed to find one." Unbelievable coincidence. Maybe. Or more likely it's a subtle nudge that you are fishing in the right direction. This random happenstance may not be so random. It might be a step in the right direction toward a door. Open doors are recognized by their ease of movement. You don't have to tear the door off of its hinges to get some movement. Open doors characterize lightness, and general positive demeanor.

You may have been told by the world that you can do anything if you have enough will power, but that isn't necessarily the case. Closed doors are repeated attempts to get closer to someone or something, and no matter what you do, it seems to blow up or go south pretty quickly. In simpler terms of my grandmother, "not meant to be." Closed doors at first, may not appear closed. But, you will eventually notice a difficulty with them. Like there's a lock-jam on the door. You start to open and it jams up. Closed doors require constant problem-solving. I guess this is the spirit's way of leading us away from something or someone that is not to be on our path. No doubt, it's not necessarily clear why. Sometimes it could take years to find out some information about why that wouldn't have been a good choice. We make choices only with the limited information we have at the time. Thank God sometimes for closed doors, and dodged bullets.

Sowing and Reaping:

I am referring to the principle of putting out in the world good energy. Good energy by helping others, assisting where needed, not making a bad situation worse by your big mouth, etc. I'm not saying we are all perfect in this venue. However, by spending the time to consider that the energy imprints we leave behind are like our DNA prints to a crime scene. How many bad actions do you want to own?

Now most people think they are relatively good people. They haven't done anything THAT bad. We generally know what that means. But you can be a buzzard from hell, big bossy mouth, that is THAT bad. You didn't kill anyone physically—just psychically or spiritually. So, you aren't a bad drunk. You don't assault people. You follow laws. In reality, though you also offend others by your constant opinions and judgments. We all have them. We might shut our mouth better if we were able to see the outcomes of some our not so great interactions. If we actually saw the imprints we left behind.

These days I joke that I must have been some kind of axe murderer in a previous lifetime. I've seen the craziest stuff. With that in mind, I like to be MORE mindful of when to have the fight, and when to realize it's not worth it. Assertiveness is a good thing for the most part. Weighing into the equation of at least leaving a situation on neutral is better than negative BECAUSE negative energy just doesn't stay put. It re-energizes and reboots itself, by itself, and takes on new victims. Forms they should never take. It's like coming home after a bad day at work, and displacing the bad energy on your partner or your dog.

The problem is that energy never actually goes away, it just changes form. The energy of a breakup of a significant relationship is still present, even moreso stronger when the person is not present. People can be broken up for seven years, and yet alive as ever in energy form. Most of us know that well. Ask anyone who has a well established drinking buddy about "that relationship" and it WILL fly out of their mouth almost uninterrupted. That relationship had a lot of energy attached to it. And then there are other relationships that leave us like flat, opened canned pop, left in the fridge too long.

Reaping, is different than sowing. Sowing is placing the order. Reaping is standing at the door when the delivery guy shows up. Most the time, we hope that we got the order in correctly, so what we receive is consistent with what we ordered. How disappointing is it when you think you ordered one thing, but the universe confused it, and gave you something else? That's how we stand and scratch our heads. Should this order be this messed up? Did I say it wrong? What got lost in translation? Am I an idiot? Is the other person the idiot?

Reaping can be very positive. Reaping can also be negative. It depends on what you've been sewing. Have you been angry? Have you been divisive? Do you lack empathy for others? Is your self-centered button always flashing? Do you talk down to people, who you think are not as successful as you? Sometimes, we all need a check-up. There are others, who are highly manipulative and have little regard for others. I don't know about you, but with those people, I just want to be present when the delivery guy shows up with their order.

The problem is that while you are waiting for someone else's karmic reaping, it's like waiting for water to boil. Geez, it should have been here by now, we think. Nope, there's no time deadlines on that stuff. Sometimes the universe wops it back fast. Other times, not so much. However, from a universal standpoint, we are constantly reaping. Reaping means collecting back either the good stuff from our interactions or the inconsiderate or worse negative stuff that's coming back again.

Of course, there's still some random things that come our way, which I believe God puts on our path to assist or cleanup with—things that make zero sense. Consider that part of universal cleanup duty. You don't know why the plastic bottles are on your lawn. You didn't throw the party or dump the garbage, but, you can be responsible for picking the junk up. Are you going to complain constantly about the junk not being yours? Or, are you going to dive in and pick it up? So, what's your sewing and reaping? What landed on you? What are you being present for? We want to be aware of what kind of energy we put out there. You can have the last word with your entitlement, but keep in mind, the universe will settle the bill. And you will pay it, one way or another.

Generational Imprints:

Imprints can have generational trickle down through our behaviors and habits, places we like to be in, etc. I think we like to think of ourselves as our own little biosphere, where we have sole independent control and our bubble is not very permeable. The good and the bad is that we are permeable.

We are made up of all these cellular computations. Habits, lifestyles, preferences, and cultural tastes, influence the way we talk, the way we walk, hand mannerisms, who our lovers are and who they are not, and mood and musical style preferences. We are constantly influencing and being influenced. Our prints are with everyone we have ever loved and everyone we did not love.

You might have acquired a generational imprint of addiction—long term alcoholism, long term drug addiction, or mind numbing fuel. You might have acquired a generational imprint of feeling neglected or abandoned. You can be the recipient of the second or third generation of "hardness." You are blessed if you are the recipient of generational love and support. Not everyone is treated with such regard. Love and support isn't about religion. It's about giving. It's about being present. Some of the biggest psychological struggles come from bitterness from a lack of regard and a lack of others to be emotionally present. Their lack becomes your lack. Often, when you look closer, there are similar roots in the way they were treated. Bad cycles. Bad energy imprints. Bad energy rebooted. These cycles need to be interrupted or changed altogether.

Relationships

We talk about people that hurt us. The problem is that you shared tight emotional or physical space with them. Mostly, we talk about people that mattered. They mattered because they were attentive. They mattered because they didn't mind your odd gestures or habits. They noticed the subtle change in your hairstyle, your half-smirk, or you let them reach over to re-adjust your clothes. We know most people by sight. However, there are that very small percentage whom you read on the inside and out. I'm talking about the super subtleties of a person that you notice. (It could be the hint of cologne in their clothes, soap, detergent, or hairspray)It's odd that we take the time with certain people to notice them at the smallest detail. And there's others, we don't care that much to do that.

The romantic kind, you borrowed their clothes and wore them to bed. The girlfriend kind, you shared your lipstick. The rebellious kind, you shared your cigarettes. The awkward intimate kind, you ate off of each-other's plate. If you really want to test a sense of intimacy, see who shares a straw on a drink. Sharing straws doesn't mean you have no options. It means you are connected.

We can gauge the closeness in relationships by the connection of some of these behaviors. The way we stand with others. The distance we keep or don't keep. The way we share or don't share personal information.

There are good solid relationships that run fairly consistently and fairly intimately in a pretty good fashion overall. They have stability. These are the types of relationships we hope to invest in. Sometimes, however, we inadvertently end up investing in relationships that don't yield any stability.

There is always a purpose to the connection, even if you have no present idea. Relationships don't always, nor are they meant to, go from birth to lifetime. Many shut down at various divinely cut points. Did you ever try to connect with someone, only to find out that your schedules always clash? That you are in one city when they are in another? If it happens once in a while; it is no big deal. If it happens frequently, that might have a divine redirection attached to it. All you really know, is that no matter what you attempt to do, you cannot reach that person. There's always a blockade of some sort. Long term relationships especially do matter, and it is often laid out that relationships come together for reason/purpose, a time in your life, or lifetime camaraderie. We can't always predict the outcome.

Intermittent reinforcement is similar to playing a slot machine. It reinforces you in sporadic format. It isn't continuous. Relationships that do THAT tend to be very addictive. You keep trying to work it out, problem-solve it, but, no matter what you do, it leaves you feeling sad and grieving. There is some relief in letting go, but it is not uncommon that these relationships can go on for years.

I would say that social media got us back in the business of old relationships or finding old soul connections. Good, bad, or indifferent, connections will always raise a certain curiosity in your mind. That curiosity may lead to further checking-in, or checking out their life. There are a small percentage of people in your life path that you will be curious about. Where that takes you, is the big question.

The divine can also put people together for greater reasons than romantic. For instance, partners such as Theodore and Eleanor Roosevelt, were initially poised for great connection perhaps because of their service based pursuits and intellectual dynamics, but biographers indicated over the years, the personal relationship had stagnated. Although the relationship supported his Presidency, there were indications that the Presidency was hard for Eleanor, as she was hoping to support some of her own projects. When your husband serves as President, First Lady obligations, and support of the President take priority. She grieved the loss of her pursuits. The point is that perhaps, the divine can indirectly or directly put different priorities in line.

Sometimes there is a different order or purpose to the cards. Some attachments will have great highs and lows, some have a great structural support, and others burn out fast.

Grief:

When the stuff that grew you..suffocates you—that's grief.

Sometimes we grieve for how things are or how things are not. What we used to be versus who we are. Grief can be at our current cards in life, current predicaments, or limitations. Grief can be over physical, tangible stuff or the intangible. The stuff that feels so important. Wounds that trigger negative emotional responses cause grief. Grief and thoughts about grief can kill people. . Or shall I say, grief and thoughts about grief can get people to kill themselves.

Grief and depression are co-partners, especially in "unresolved" or "traumatic" grief. The people who are suffering grief and loss in great waves, for years at a time, where they fail to stabilize and rebuild from.

Faulty biochemistry is responsible for the severe drop off in functioning that occurs when depression or Bipolar co-mingle with grief. One minute a person is managing their grief, and at another time, they are feeling it so strongly AND it doesn't improve. Depression or Bipolar magnifies the intensity of the grief. What most professionals do not know is that mood disorders are the RIPTIDE below the surface that makes grief become complicated and go unresolved for years. Many assume the sadness is just coming from grief alone, and will not search for an underlying mood condition. So basically, the person never really gets "over it."

Grief comes in many forms. In the field of Psychology, there are books about stages of grief that many people are familiar with. AS IF people will just follow this recipe of grief symptoms, and eventually come out the other end. In my work, I rarely see it work like that. I see some of those elements present with each different type of grief, but not necessarily a "working order" that heals people. I think people heal grief. I think relationships and support heals grief. Whether a person is able to be open to that or not, is a whole different story. I no longer believe the stages are relevant, other than in helping a person understand they are involved in a grief process. What matters is their ability to make some kind of connection to keep some type of hope alive in their life. When there is no connection and a person is surrounded by loss and decay: watch out, there is a very good potential that person may take their own life. Life is about hope and the ability to have some positive purpose. The problem is that a person who is surrounded by a profound sense of loss and decay doesn't necessarily inform others about it. Once that interpersonal hope cannot be reconstructed or affirmed, there is serious risk. Lack of investment might add to this. It can be described as little interest in daily activities, as simple as bathing or eating properly. Behind every depressed person, I find a level or style of grief. Grief and depression coexist in a bad way, like drug dealers and drugs. The relationship is there—it's just not a good one.

Depression or Bipolar spectrum is the equivalent of putting gas heat under a pot. It gets the grief to a peak boiling point; where there is severe inability to cope. If you don't understand the nature of these two pieces working in tandem, then you are missing a lot of information. Let me say this again, specifically for anyone who believes that grief just operates in isolation.

If a person has a biological predisposition to depression or Bipolar, their disposition will magnify the intensity and duration of the grief. This unresolved or "traumatic grief" can cause a person to be in therapy for years, with LITTLE to show for it. Depression, Bipolar II, Bipolar I, or Bipolar spectrum act like a great elevator drop in the ability to regulate the mood, which in turn, makes the grief response very reactive. In other words, first the mood disorder needs to be better regulated; if you would like to see any improvement in a person's grief response. An analogy to this is; no use in cleaning the deck of the boat every time a wave comes, if the engine propeller isn't fastened in properly. Without the propeller being fastened in properly, the boat will keep taking on unnecessary waves.

A SENSE OF FAILURE:

Nothing builds gloom and doom better and faster than a sense of failure. What do you think you failed at? What lies do you believe about this failure? Even though you may be obsessively thinking about how you've messed up, there is always a Plan B. We have a problem with Plan B, because we believe that Plan A was perfect for what we needed. Plan B does not feel good. Plan B comes with guilt, sadness, shame, loss, etc. Who the hell orders Plan B? Simply stated, no one. Plan B shows up often unannounced. You are lucky if you get a bit of a memo or a sign beforehand. Plan B scenarios are often trials. Are you a bit surprised by the trials you have faced? Are there other Plan B's that you did well with? Keep in mind, there's also trials that you dodged inadvertently, that you really didn't know about.

Plan A may have been our first choice, but being forced into Plan B sometimes takes us into richer opportunity than we ever imagined.

FAILING CAN BE AN INSIDE TRACK TO SUCCESS:

If you are going to live well, then you have to know how to fail and take a hit. What this teaches us, is how to rework our thought process. It teaches you how to change our thinking in the face of failure. If you have always been a perfectionist, that just tells me that you hide behind the wall, when the game of dodge ball starts. To get any points in the game of life, you have to know how to throw the ball back. Hiding is temporary security. Hiding behind someone else or something else is not a long term strategy. It's a short term one. Eventually, you have to learn to grab a ball, hurl it, and keep moving. You can't sit still or hide in the line when the balls start flying.

People like the security of numbers. Numbers in the red are bad, numbers in the black are good. We are constantly inter-preting numbers. We like to hide behind the numbers of pop-ular opinion. That's nice, but that's not living. Numbers invite you to be a sheep. Sheep is a good thing. They get along, they are positive, but they don't pursue anything independently. That's why there's always a sheep herder. Black sheep get heck-led early on. They are visibly different. Their differentness will one day prove to be an asset. Their differentness pushes them to the outer curve. They may at first hit the rail, but over time, they learn to find the draft (the person or situation) that propels them to access speed and forward momentum.

People who can follow rules, but also know when to step out of the box, are usually very successful. Why? Because they aren't waiting for a standing ovation for their efforts. They focus on getting past issues. They problem-solve. They also know when and how to disagree internally and rework their thought patterns to keep going. Just because someone says it cannot be done, doesn't make it true. Movement, even small movement, is the key to making change. Eventually, small subtle movements, key up to larger movements. We can build on small. We just can't build on absence. Sheep don't build. Sheep follow. If you are different or are going to be different, than you don't get the comfort of being a sheep. Ultimately, though, the constant discomfort you face eventually introduces you to your real space. Your unique gifting. So take heart, if you are not a sheep, you were never intended to be one. You were supposed to be different and likely land a bigger space.

SELF ESTEEM WAKE UP CALL:

People use the term in a global fashion. Like you either have self-esteem or you don't have any. I completely disagree with this concept. Self-esteem is not an all or nothing concept, that people try to convince you of on a daily basis. Instead of "she has low self-esteem," try instead, "she has some areas of her life, that she does not feel confident about currently." If you have mega self-esteem, it's likely that you have never been tested hard in life. As people get tested, they get more humble even with their success. Successful people know in life they are successful, because they've had to take some hard knocks, some hard decisions, and some losses. Success isn't one big clapping party.

For instance, in most people's lives, there are areas that a person feels that they are very competent. This may be at work, school, or at domestic tasks. There is an area, that no matter what or how you are feeling, you know that you are good at accomplishing certain types of things. You don't need anyone to tell you. Just like kids, they will tell you if they are good at math, or good at spelling. They just know.

When a person is lacking self-esteem, options often include buying new clothes and draping yourself in the best stuff. That may briefly lift you, but it won't lift you long. That's why you have to keep buying more stuff. You also may have to be surrounding yourself with others who have more than you. The more internalized your self-esteem becomes, the less you need on the outside. You can live in a teepee, smell like a hog, and feel confident about yourself, because what you really need is internal.

So, when someone says, "I have low self-esteem," I ask more targeted questions. Ultimately, the person feels good or competent in certain areas and not so competent in others. An all or nothing rating system works well with having a disease or not having the disease, but it is rarely accurate in describing a person's self-esteem and sense of self-competence.

What biochemical self-esteem can look like…

I believe that self-esteem fluctuates according to mood. If a person's serotonin level (calmness) is tumbling down, their thinking becomes negative, self-attacking, and obsessive. So, not only will they experience a negative mood, but their thought system will likely also become depressed. The person will have a hard time in their own head, and likely not want to be around others. When we cannot deal with ourselves, most of us do not want the ADDED stress of dealing with others. Therefore, a person with relatively good self-esteem can choose to isolate and report not feeling good about themselves. How does that happen? It can happen because of the internal chemistry is not where it needs to be, and a person will experience depression, anxiety and self-consciousness.

A simple trip to the grocery store can prove a panicky and overwhelming experience for them that no one can really explain.

In contrast, when a person is taking Opiates or Amphetamines, levels of norepinephrine and dopamine are raised and the sense of self-esteem switches to positive. The person exhibits a "can do" space. Noone who takes stimulants feels like a failure and shuts down. If anything, they are visible, and feel more confident, at least temporarily. This is why the drug trade is as big as it is. It is instant, but not long lasting—self-esteem can be temporarily achieved, on a line, in a bottle, or in a needle.

Self-esteem, and the ability of a person to be outgoing and social, is largely influenced by the INTERNAL chemical equation. In usual circumstances, if a person has depression or anxiety, they will experience more difficulty putting themselves out in the world. They would feel more shaky, self-conscious, or nervous and tend towards isolation. Their self-esteem would appear low. However, when biochemistry levels off, they tend to become more outgoing and social. From the outside, it can look very confusing. How can a person who is usually social and confident, tend to shut down and isolate? If the biochemistry is shaky on the inside, it will dictate heavily whether a person can socialize or withdraw.

Unfortunately, people RARELY ever recognize the INTERNAL equation that is imposing on the external ability to put themselves out there.

HOPELESSNESS:

It is the invisible factor that drains life out of a soul. Hopeless can happen with a Stage IV illness. It can happen with the loss of an important relationship. It can happen with traumatic wounds. Life without hope becomes an existence problem.

Hope is what makes life interesting and adds zest and purpose. Hope is energy and zeal.

Hopelessness is not tangible. It's not something you can readily see, but it reveals itself by what is NOT happening in a person's world. If a person stagnates, meaning they no longer reach out on the phone, they do not go to work, and they do not involve themselves in any meaningful pursuit, then there is a very good chance that hopelessness is present. It may not come out in direct conversation, but if you look around you will find evidence of it. Clothes all over, dishes in the sink, wrappers, papers, alcohol, cigarettes, missing appointments, calling in for work, and no food in the fridge, these are all potential signs that someone is not functioning.

The next question is what do you do when hopelessness is suspect? Any small agreeable movement matters. It may matter, just that you are willing to be present with them. When hopelessness is a factor, people usually have something stuck in their head that they can't let go of. It can also be a relationship that is no longer in their life. If you can't get them to talk, try to get them to someone who can be present for them like a therapist. Offer to take them there. Help fill in gaps by getting them to eat. Try to get them to join in or bringing a person to outside activity—whether to meet for coffee, attend a class together, or attend a group session. Help them neutralize any potential failure they see themselves to be, or mistakes, or judgments they have towards themselves. Professionals are your best bet, if the person is willing to seek out therapy. Just be an additional support to the professional. Do not just dump them off with a therapist. Monitor them for suicidal ideation. Alert any professional of these concerns. If there isn't any professional available, take them to an ER, and they will proceed with obtaining a Psychiatric assessment.

Who Are People Who Are At Risk For Suicide...

Check for hopelessness. Hopelessness is a huge factor. Does the situation feel permanent? Check for a traumatic event. Note people who have PTSD from witnessing or being a part of a traumatic event are very much at risk. This includes war veterans. A present example of this, is people who have experienced shootings. People often speak of survivor guilt as a factor. But a commonly overlooked factor are traumatic flashbacks at night, nightmares, or night terrors. Unfortunately, there is a significant correlation between nightmares and suicide attempts. If sleep is seriously compromised, so is healing. Many people don't talk about nightmares, but experience extreme distress from them, especially if they have flashbacks attached to them. The next piece to look at is associational triggers. These are associations that are linked even loosely to the traumatic event. A person may experience looking at something as simple as a chair and begin to re-experience trauma. So, often times it is not just the trauma event itself, but also the associations that are triggering as well. The trauma event then goes tentacles.

According to Littlewood, DL, Gooding, PA, Panagioti M. Kyle SD, "Nightmares and suicide in Posttraumatic Stress Disorder: the mediating role of defeat, entrapment, and hopelessness". *Journal of Clinical Sleep Medicine* 2016; 12(3):393-399. "Nightmares act as a stressor and directly trigger perceptions of defeat."

In *Scientific American MIND*, "Mental Health, Nightmares May Signal Increased Risk of Suicide", Carr, Michelle, January 1, 2017. In research evaluating suicide risk in undergraduates, and how anxiety, depression, and nightmares were related to the risk. "Having nightmares correlated with overall suicide risk more closely than any other factor."

What can be done? Eye Movement Desensitization Retraining can assist with reducing effects of trauma. As trauma is reduced, hopelessness tends to reduce. When people feel like they can escape chronic feelings of being trapped in a trauma mindset, hope can be restored.

Psychology often calls upon multiple interventions including the use of interpersonal supports, which is critical. Therapy is implemented to help the person manage and reconfigure defective thought patterns. Psychiatry is useful for medication management to help the brain re-calibrate its baseline. Most importantly, you need to be a team player. Recognize the strength in numbers and be direct with different types of supports.

Diathesis: Stress Model

What makes any disease visible is a medical predisposition that gets added to stress. We all carry genes for certain predispositions or genetic limitations. The Diathesis Stress model basically states that we have wired in weaknesses that have been genetically transferred. There are things that can be done to stabilize these traits, such as taking vitamin supplements, using exercise as a joint preventative, or alkaline diets to ward of cancer, etc. We may never experience many of these medical weaknesses because of internal changes or an external buffer stops the thread from unraveling. The problem happens when multiple risk patterns that stress can provide outweigh the vulnerability. Stress is used as a mild word, but there's nothing mild about its effects.

Stress that's placed on the brain becomes stress that eventually overtakes the body with disease. According to Harvard Health Publishing, "Understanding the Stress Response," updated 5/1/18, with original publication March 2011, "research suggests that chronic stress contributes to high blood pressure, promotes the formation of artery clogging deposits, and causes brain changes that may contribute to anxiety, depression, and addiction." When the brain has to constantly release stress chemicals, that keep the body on high alert; it's like running your body like a drag car—too much energy surge. The organs are the mechanical system that get put under vigilant attack. Eventually parts wear out and break down. The blood stream can get clogged with dirt and debris. Over time, we become exposed to a disease process.

If you have ever had a panic attack, or got stuck with an epi pen, you have felt the effects of an adrenaline surge. When your body does it by itself, in an uncalculated way: you are now exposed to fight or flight. The brain and body rely on the HPA system to make all of that happen. The fight or flight system was set up initially for survival. Basically, it's like what nitrous does for drag cars. It gives you energy when you need it most. It comes in handy if you have to lift a car off of a child, run from a wild beast, or fight for your life. However, if the situation is not life-threatening, it is a rather uncomfortable power surge in the system. We all presume that our brain communicates with our body in an effective manner. However, when levels dip or surge out too high, then the physiological effects can feel overwhelming.

HPA Axis and the Sympathetic Nervous System:

HPA refers to the Hypothalamus-Pituitary-Adrenal connection, which is triggered under stress. According to Harvard

Health Publishing, "Understanding the Stress Response," as cited above, the amygdala, which is part of the HPA axis receives threat alert. Once the amygdala fires, it triggers the Hypothalamus. The Hypothalamus is referred to as the "command center" and communicates with the rest of the body through the Sympathetic and Parasympathetic functions of the Autonomic Nervous System. Body functions such as breathing, heart rate, and blood pressure are kept on alert. Priority is given to survival mechanisms (glucose availability) rather than more passive functions such as digestion. The hypothalamus triggers the pituitary (the master) organizer to release chemicals in the system that trigger the release of hormones, which provide detailed code information. The endocrine system triggers the adrenal glands that release stress hormones such as cortisol. Build up of excess cortisol can cause weight gain and diabetes. According to "Cortisol—Its Role in Stress, Inflammation, and Indications for Diet Therapy" by Aronson, Dina, MS, RD, *Today's Dietician* Vol. 11 No. 11. p. 38, "when chronically elevated, cortisol can have deleterious effects of weight, immune function, and chronic disease risk." "Cortisol (along with its partner epinephrine) is best known for its involvement in the fight or flight response and temporary increase in energy production, at the expense of processes that are not required for immediate survival." What this means is that going into a chronic state of stress, frequently or prolonged, is going to have negative physiological consequences, and eventually, cumulatively impact the body as a whole. So, if you find that you get ill relatively easily, then it's likely that you run your body under a chronic stress state. Chronic stress creates all kinds of immune system problems and autoimmune diseases.

When you are trying, but something isn't working…

A common response that I've heard is "I've been taking an antidepressant." Some people are taking two. The reality is whatever you are taking, that chemistry is not working properly, or the boat would not keep taking on large waves. You may be working on a fix, but the diagnostics are probably wrong. Maybe your depression or anxiety is really more of a Bipolar spectrum. Maybe it hovers in cycles or maybe it has a steep surge or down surge to it. It just makes it hard to manage other things.

Bipolar depression or Bipolar anxiety causes wave-like instability. It doesn't matter who you are. If you were to take your white blood cell count and triple it, the response is going to be a fever and lethargy. Fever doesn't discriminate based on who you are. It's a medical alarm system. Similarly, chemical neurotransmitters establish mood, if mood doesn't reasonably calibrate it is also a medical alarm system.

When mood gets lower, it causes tearfulness and obsessive thinking, which is consistent with serotonin drop off. The person's thoughts are dark, hopeless, and repetitive. If there is a lot of thought energy present, then it just keeps going and going, like a hamster on a rat wheel. At those times, the person feels completely overwhelmed, and feels as if they will "never" get over their grief. They have good reason to feel this way. Since the overwhelming mood state has likely been ineffectively treated for years. The grief just walked in and aggravated an already difficult biochemistry. The overwhelming mood state is reenergizing all the thoughts about grief. Any person who experiences this type of experience can improve significantly, if the possibility of a severe mood disorder or Bipolar depression is recognized and treated through a Psychiatrist or a Psychiatric nurse practitioner, as well as treating the negative thought process that is also fueling it through counseling.

BLOCKADES TO THOUGHT WORK:

Positive thinking is important. Certainly, a person can start to learn to train their thinking into more positive modes. It is important to understand that for some people, it is more difficult than it is for others. A person who comes from a family who has a genetic history of depression has a high likelihood of the presence of that gene. What that means, is that the person's normal starting point, is going to be emotionally lower than where it should be. The chemical equation is shorted a bit. For example, if you are 5 ft. 10 inches and you are playing basketball against an opponent who is 6ft. 4inches, you are up against a significant disadvantage. Obviously, the 6ft. 4inch person has height with less proximal range to shoot from, larger hands to reach and block, fewer strides across the court, and a wider range advantage. The only disadvantage is if the 6ft 4 inch person has no motor skills, where they lack the fast foot work, lack cardio, and body work to coordinate to get the ball in the basket. Generally, however, head to head, it will be much easier for the 6 ft. 4 inch person, presuming they have motor skills to make the basket. Again, if the baseline of feeling good is at 70, but your genetic wiring brings you in at best at a 55, you are going to have to work harder emotionally and physically to bridge that gap. This is important because many people presume that everyone has the same chemical wiring with the same set point. Altering your thinking slightly with good results is positive. If you are trying to change your thinking, but your chemical foundation does not stand firm (like riding a small wave), then the degree of difficulty is not the same. The person who experiences depression or anxiety will struggle harder to improve their thinking because the foundation base has a lower starting point.

SET POINT THEORY:

Set point theory from a medical standpoint discusses how your bodyweight and temperature like to stabilize around a certain point. The set point theory of one's mood is the tendency for mood to stabilize around a certain constant. Like IQ, this tends to exhibit stability over time. Set point theory of happiness includes personality traits that are inborn and those that are prone to a fixed range of variability.

For example, the young child who parents report "has no fear." That trait tends to stick over time. The child will be looking for adrenaline based activities and will be likely to engage in higher risk behaviors and impulse styled responses. A "thrill-seeking" extraverted personality is likely to remain relatively fixed. Similarly, a child who hides behind the parent's legs to peek out and view the world, this child exhibits a cautious, guarded, anxious style of interacting. The behavior may modify to a certain extent, but the trait stays relatively stable. You will not live to see this child engage in socially reckless behavior.

Genetics is the pre-wiring that is fixed in your brain (like the hardware to the computer). You can modify the brain with different types of interventions (software), but the baseline hardware is where the brain likes to return. Essentially, this is it's default function. The setpoint is a biological code that is derived from chemical equations and genetic inheritance.

There are fact-based, science-based types of thinkers versus creative, artistic, and emotionally tapped thinkers. There is no right or wrong in these styles. However, it's more like the known information in a geometry problem. Hard science thinkers are not prone to strong emotional expression any more than persons prone to artistic expression are interested in using algorithms to solve mechanical equations.

When you examine mood, you also need to examine your relatives' mood and behavior response styles. Unfortunately, with person's who commit suicide there are other relatives who have done the same. Suicide tends to carry related or relative genetic risk. Being more specific, the depression that causes suicidal activity tends to run in families. According to Ping Qin, MD, PhD "The Relationship of Suicide Risk to Family History of Suicide and Psychiatric Disorders (Dec1, 2003), *Psychiatric Times,* "Family history of suicide and mental or substance abuse disorder are among the most prevalent risk factors for suicide in the United States." Keep in mind that it is not a one to one relationship, but it is one very high risk factor. Mental health factors such as mood, thought patterns, and personality styles can influence these outcomes.

From a common sense viewpoint, optimists tend to carry a higher than average more positive view of the world. Pessimists, in contrast tend to view situations with more loaded potential for negativity. Genetic set point helps establish these baselines.

Just because you have the set point does not guarantee the same outcome. Modifying different variables in the medical, social, and environmental model is important.

THINKING CONSIDERATIONS:

Even if you have a lowered set point, there is still plenty you can do to assist in improving your thought process. Improving your thinking will improve your ability to cope and problem-solve. Greasing one part of the machine will ease up the mechanics on the other part of brain functioning.

For instance, have you ever found yourself extremely upset while trying to figure something out? Unexpectedly, someone introduces a different concept, and then you are able to reconfigure your problem. Sometimes, we don't need an entire overhaul, we just need to understand a part of the equation that is getting stuck.

In Psychology, Cognitive Behavioral therapy is used to help a person recognize extreme or ineffective ways of thinking. Bad or ineffective thinking causes bad behavioral responses and a faulty sense of self-perception. We can get lost in perception completely at the gate.

You can get it all written down, organized, and temporarily internally reworked. At the end of it all, your brain segues into trying to understand the hard hits in your life.

You don't learn how to box outside the arena. You have to step in IT. To get a mood disorder of any type improved, you have to be willing to take a look at it. You have to be willing to see that there are medical factors in the equation. You have to be willing to see that there are Psychological factors in the mix as well. To get better, you have to trust some professionals in the process. This doesn't have to be a big deal. At first, you watch and then you have to know something about the punches, the positioning, how they work, before you learn how to duck, and do a side step, and avoid the incoming punch.

You can get better faster, but you have to study your body, to start figuring out HOW the medical factors tie in, and what physical or emotional features present next, does it cycle, or is it a low swing or drop?

Isolating, drinking to excess, getting by with your job only barely, can keep this process in play for years. Dare to be bolder and smarter than that. When you are smart enough to know it doesn't feel right, don't keep doing what isn't working. Don't abuse substances and exist in a circle of trying to bring down too high of a high, or bring up a too low of a low. Realize that this is fixable. It's not just existable. Don't listen to the ship of fools of too many messed up people with bad habits or judgments who never help.

Learning how to change some of your thinking, correct it, or detangle it from your past is critical. Recognizing how biochemical shifts play a role in that is important. Just thinking positive on its own merit is a LOT hard to do, especially when your chemical levels bungee drop. If your levels don't do the bungee drop, then it will be a lot easier to self-correct, or think positive…build your future…imagine your best self. When you get a chemical platform to stand on, then you can go bigger and better with your thought process. Just finding another job, another relationship, or moving to another place, is not going to fix the chemical equation.

Spiritual Depression:

Spiritual depression isn't actually a formal diagnosis, but I think it makes sense to a lot of people. Depression in your spirit is when your spirit is just beat up, and you don't feel positive about life. It could be about one event in your life, or it can be about several. When you don't understand why you have to endure all sorts of hardship. It's what happens when a rogue wave hits and disorients your plan of expectation.

When you take a lot of different directions, but hope or positivity is not on the radar.

Over time, spiritual depression is just as hard on the body as anything else stress related. The stress responses start to fire. Stress happens when what we think will fix it, doesn't. The answers you had are just that. You had them. Hence, the supportive biochemistry in your body may start to falter, and you can start to develop a chemical imbalance in the process—especially if you can't get your 4WD back in the game.

When your spirit gets low, you need to find people that understand you—people who are safe; people who are real and not intimidated by much. You need certified boxers in the ring. To get certified in something, you have to have some experience with it. This is why A. A. does so well. Recovery based addicts reaching out. They speak the language. When the language is understood, you get better faster. Celebration Recovery, often available in larger non-denominational churches, helps in aiding in substance abuse support as well.

What to Do:

There are natural supplements that help with mood support. Vitamin B Complex (liquid), liquid tends to have better absorption than tablets. The B vitamins are very helpful with mood, more specifically B6, and B12. Niacin (flush free) is helpful for depression and anxiety, Fish Oil (Omega 3's), and Vitamin D3.

You can also build serotonin, norepinephrine, and dopamine neurotransmitters by eating certain foods. You may find the same by searching foods that build serotonin, foods that build norepinephrine, etc.

Pharmaceutical medications for depression, anxiety, or Bipolar generally fall within three camps. The antidepressants which offer the SSRI's (build serotonin), SNRI's (build norepinephrine), SNDI's (build norepinephrine & dopamine). The anti-anxiety meds are Xanax, Ativan, and Klonopin. These are closely monitored due to addiction potential and are usually best for short-term use. There are also the mood stabilizers that are helpful for regulating mood for Bipolar depression or manic anxiety. It is imperative to have a Psychiatrist or Psychiatric Nurse Practitioner, assist with discussing questions or concerns. Have a therapist assist with coping patterns to help assist in re-regulating your thought process. If you can start re-regulating your thought process, then you can start improving your mood by neutralizing thoughts that break you down or give way to failure.

What I've attempted to bring to the forefront are different ways to get information and start healing. Figuring out where you are most stuck. There's the biology of the individual to take into account, and then there's the psychological patterns, the way in which someone thinks, but also there is the spirit factor of the individual.

I have stressed integrating the importance of a medical model in understanding mood disorders and the biochemistry or neural factors that cause them. I have also tried to explain personality disorders in an easier way, and personal and inter-personal factors that effect these dynamics.

The journey can be rugged, but it is worthy. I have walked this path with many people. You can do this. If you found this book by accident; maybe it wasn't an accident.

Fix your outward face, fix your rudder, and adjust your sails. It can get good again.